FROM
HERE
— TO —
THERE

VERONICA

authorHOUSE®

AuthorHouse™
1663 Liberty Drive
Bloomington, IN 47403
www.authorhouse.com
Phone: 833-262-8899

Published by AuthorHouse 07/05/2022

ISBN: 978-1-6655-6122-8 (sc)
ISBN: 978-1-6655-6121-1 (e)

Library of Congress Control Number: 2022910370

Print information available on the last page.

Any people depicted in stock imagery provided by Getty Images are models, and such images are being used for illustrative purposes only.
Certain stock imagery © Getty Images.

This book is printed on acid-free paper.

CONTENTS

INTRODUCTION

This book is about times and events in my life that I wanted to share with my readers.

My name is Veronica. I come from a family of twelve; six sisters and five brothers. My mother was the mother of fourteen. She raised all twelve of us to see adulthood. We were a close-knit family coming up. Over the years many things have changed but God is large and in charge. I am number eight in the bunch. My mom said I was the nosy one in the family because I was always asking questions why this is and why that. She sometimes just smiled and told me that there are things you do not need to know right now. I am the mother of one daughter, Delilah, and the proud grandmother of five grandchildren. I have three granddaughters April, Shannon, and Anastasia. My two grandsons are Princeton and Sloan. I cannot leave my son-n-law Maximillian out whom I love like my own son.

LOOKING BACK ON MY LIFE

I am looking back to the age of five walking down the hall in the house where we use to live. This house was an apartment house that had a long hallway that separated the two living spaces. We lived in the apartment to the right and our neighbors, the Hills, who was also our cousins lived in the one to our left. There was the mother, Ms. Hattie, and she had seven children. There was four boys Ben, Ron, Jim, and Will. The three girls were Faye, Betty, and Sally. There were three other girls that lived out of state. There was always something going on in that two-part apartment We were always into it about something. There was twelve of us, so we were the larger family and I often look back with a question in my mind of how did we all stay in that tiny space? My mom and stepdad were Mr. and Mrs. Wilson. The six sisters were Wilma, Stella, Bell, Millie, Clara, and Asley. Wilma was the oldest, then Stella, Bell, Millie, Clara, and Ashley were the baby. The five boys were Pete, Jerry, Russel, Jack, and Walter. Pete was the oldest, then Jerry, Russel,

Jack, and Walter was the baby boy. There was a long porch that reached from one side of the apartment house to the other. We loved to sit on that porch and watch the rain on rainy days. We had good neighbors, of course, that was back when you did not have to lock your door. When the whole village raised the children. The days when everyone showed love to everyone and everyone visited each other, laugh, and talk and had a good time. All the children would get together and play all day long. I never remembered a disagreement between neighbors back then. You could just feel the love. What happened to those days?

There was a store down the street that we use to go to. The lady that owned the store was Ms. German. We spent so much money at that store; we were always there. Ms. German had a dog she kept behind the counter that got out sometimes. I was so afraid of that dog. I did not know what kind of dog he was as a little girl but looking back I know he was a bulldog. He was so big to me! There was a neighbor down the street that had a dog that like to run you. This lady's name was Ms. Ruth Long, and her dogs named was Bootsy. She was always out walking her dog.

The neighbors that lived next door to us became good friends with my mom and stepdad. Let me explain why I keep saying stepdad. My mom was married twice. My mom had eight children by my dad and four by my stepdad. I am the eighth child, my dad's baby. My mom said my stepdaddy raised me from six months old. Now, back to our next-door neighbor. My sister Bell and I was so much of a tom-boy that we played marbles with the boys in the neighborhood. The boys always stayed mad with us because we would win all their marbles. Bruce liked to shoot marbles and we stayed in his yard all the time. Like I said before our parents had become good friends. His parents were Bruce and Marilyn Jones. I believe Mr. Jones was a taxi driver. Mrs. Marilyn stayed home. My mom and stepdad worked but I can not remember them not working. I remember the day that Bruce bit my sister Bell on her lips. She came in the house hollering and screaming like crazy. My mom asked her what happened, and she said she did not know. Mom said well he had to have his lips on your lips for him to bite you. Life on Field Street was very memorable. Mr. Bruce and Mrs. Marilyn had daughters as well; one of them was named Jackie. I never knew of any other brothers.

There was Ms. Raye and her son Ryan. They were noticeably quiet people. I can count on my hand the times I saw either of them. They did not sit out or talk to anybody. I could often remember the times I could see them watching tv in their house. I never saw anybody that came to visit or anything. Looking back, they acted as if they were hiding something like a witness protection program or something. All I know they were very unusual people. However, the times that I did see them they would always speak when I spoke to them.

Mr. and Mrs. Green was also neighbors of ours. They sat on the porch all the time. Mrs. Green was always home, but Mr. Green would always go to town. He scooted around on his hands. He had a special device that he used to protect his knees or bottom. He did not let being disabled stop him. He sold stuff downtown on the streets. I think one of them was peanuts. They were nice people, never heard anything about them after we moved.

There was Ms. Maude, here daughter and two sons. The sons were Don, John, and Robin her daughter. They were also quiet people. I never saw any of them until they were leaving home. They always walked pass the house and were friendly people too. Years after moving off that street I ended up working in the school system with John.

Then there was Mr. Johnson. He had his picks and chooses. My brother worked in his yard for him. That was the first time I heard the word 'color struck.' One day my brother Russel was stung by some wasps. Russel was darker skin than my brother Jerry. Mom said Mr. Johnson was color struck because he laughed at Russel and told him the reason he was stung was because the wasp could not see Jerry in the day light. Mom said he said, "get him, a black rascal!' He did not want Russel to come in the house but would let Jerry in. My mom stopped them both from going to his house. I think I would have done the same thing. You did not mistreat my mom's children. There was a café downtown named 'Johnson.' I wonder if he owned it. I never heard anything else about him.

Ms. Mildred and her daughters, Pam and Lela stayed around the corner. That was the first time I heard my mom and stepfather have cross words. My mom and Ms. Mildred had it out too. I remember my mom saying something about Ms. Mildred was always in my stepdad's face. My stepdad was just sitting there looking at my mom. He got so quiet after a while. Mom was talking about going around the corner whipping this lady's butt. Whatever was going on it soon smoothed over. I never saw them over on our street again, so I did not know much about them. We managed to stay connected over the years on Facebook. We also would see each other from time to time. My mom was a beautiful person inside and out. Everybody loved her; they called her Sweetie. So, what ever happened in this situation must have really been something.

Ms. Betty and Ms. Nancy stayed in the alley behind our house. They were sisters and both had blue hair and blue eyes. I was so afraid of them. I thought they were witches. I found out later that they sold moonshine. There was always a lot of people going down that alley. I do not know if they ever got any sleep.

Ms. Margaret lived next door to the left of us. She took care of all her grands. She had a grandson whose name was Jim. Jim always dressed in her clothes and heels parading up and down the street. Back then that was not cool, so he was talk of all the neighbors. He talked back to Ms. Margaret like she was a child. I do not know what happened to Him after we left Field Street. I did hear that they sent him north to live with family. I often wonder if that was a good thing or not. Ms. Mildred had a granddaughter that had a crush on my brother Jack. She was always talking to him from across the yard. She wanted Jack to come over to her house. I do not think he ever went.

There was this big house across the street. I did not know what kind of house it was because there were a lot of people there all the time. This house had a porch that went all the way around it with lots of doors in it. I found out years later it was not a good place. Ms. Edna was the lady that ran the house. I do not have to tell you what kind of house that was. How I found out was years later after my sister Wilma started working there. I often saw her walking around that porch. When I found out what went on in there I was like WOW! I do not think that the neighbors cared anything about this lady and the things she was doing. I know that the alley beside that house was a short-cut to town. WOW!

Dr. Williams was the doctor everyone in the neighborhood used because he was a block away. Everyone liked Dr. Williams because he was always there for them. We never had to go to the doctor because my mom believed in home remedies. If we went to the doctor, it was because we had to go for something like stepping on a nail or something similar. Right before winter set in mom would give us Castrol, 666, and Scott Emulsion. Dr. Williams remained my doctor long after we left Field Street. There was talk about a girl that died under his care. That rumor was spoken of for years but later the truth came out that the girl died from fat that covered her heart. People are so quick to judge. I never heard anything else about it after that. Dr. Williams in my book was an awesome doctor.

Ms. Mary was an old lady that lived across the street. She told everything on everybody. Everybody called her nosy. Ms. Mary and my mom later gave me that same name because she said I asked a lot of questions. Ms. Mary would fall out with everybody on that street from time to time. She would cook cakes and call my cousin Sally from next door to get a cake. She told her not to give Sweetie's children none of it. She would be upset with my mom when she did things like that. My cousin always shared with us anyway that is the way we were. We looked out for each other. Ms. Mary fell one day, and my stepdad laughed at her. Mom told him he was so wrong for that. He laughed out loud at her. I remember that day like it was yesterday. Mom went over to check on her. I do not think she had any family; I never saw anyone. She was an old lonesome lady and she thought she was looking out for everyone by staying in their business. I do know we knew to respect here. That is the way mom brought us up.

Mom had a friend, Mr. Carl, who came by the house all the time, he was so loud. He always visited the ladies' house in the alley behind us. They were known in the neighborhood as bootleggers. Whenever he returned from the house in the alley, everybody in the house would get up to see what all the noise was coming from. Mr. Carl would come back drunk all the time. After I was born, mom said he came to the door and looked at me in her arms and started screaming, "Oh Lord, Mrs. Wilson done had a white baby." He went down the street saying it over and over again. Mom told him to stop saying that because that was not true even though everybody in the neighborhood knew she worked for a white man. She said Mr. Carl was crazy. I do remember seeing him pass by our house falling down drunk, but I never saw a police officer stop him. I never heard anything else about Mr. Carl after we left Field St.

I remember walking down the hall one day when I heard a noise coming from my mom's room. I peeped in the door and caught my brother Jerry stealing cigarettes from my mom's purse. I was always catching those brothers of mine. He tried to bribe me not to tell mom. "I'll take you to the movies if you don't tell mom," he said. I said ok, so he took me to the movie, and he also made me a necklace. He was my favorite brother, but I still told on him. If my mom had not been fussing that day about somebody was taking cigarettes from her pack, I never would have told it. I said it before I knew it. Jerry was so upset with me. I believe mom already knew that those older brothers were taking her cigarettes. One thing we did not do was to argue, fuss or fight. Disrespect was forbidden in my mom's house. All she had to do was look at you. She had a dangerous look. You knew to straighten up and fly right. Those were the words my mom always used.

The house we lived in had wood floors that you could practically look through the cracks. You could see the ground through some of the planks. Mom used to be a smoker. I remember her giving my sister Stella a cigarette butt to put out and she dropped it down in a crack in the floor and almost set the house on fire. You should have seen everyone; we were getting water and pouring it down through that crack in the floor. It was a scary moment. Mom told us that she believed Stella was trying to smoke the butt from the cigarette. I would say that Stella has been smoking since she was seven years old. Mom also said she suspected she was one of the ones taking cigarettes out of her purse. Stella was always doing weird stuff. We were sitting in the front room one day and mom liked drinking water out of a tin can because the older people said it is the coldest water you would want to drink. That day mom sent Stella to get her some water and commented how good and cold the water was and sent Stella at some more. Mom asked the oldest sister to follow her to see where she was getting the water from and Wilma came running and hollering, "Stella is getting that water out of a bucket!"

Mom said, "Oh Lord" what? Mom instantly got sick and was sick for a week or more. She could not eat or drink a thing. We felt so bad for mom. She said she was not going to whip her for it, she just knew not to send her to do nothing else.

My grandpa came to live with us. Grandpa was mom's mother's daddy. Grandpa was always gone to town, and we knew when he came back that he had something for all his grandchildren. Grandpa walked with a walking stick, and we would all wait, listening for the sound of grandpa's walking stick hitting the wood floor. We would all race to him, just so anxious and grandpa would pass the bag and tell us to take it to Mom. I guess grandpa said it was too many of us coming at him at one time.

He had the biggest cigar hanging out of his mouth. I cannot remember ever seeing it lit. Now that I think about it, he was using it for a taste of tobacco. It always caught my attention. Everybody knew grandpa by name, Frank Wilson. One day after grandpa made it home, he went to his room and about an hour later we heard a big boom. It sounded like the biggest boom I had ever heard. Mom told all of us to stay put and do not move. Unknowingly grandpa had just died in the bathroom. The reason I knew it was the bathroom was because my mom kept a number three tin tub in there. That was the loud noise we heard. Grandpa must have hit the tub when he fell. All my siblings were sitting looking at each other. Mom came back to the room and said grandpa just died, she was terribly upset and crying. We all started crying too, we loved our grandpa. If a hearse came to pick up his body, I would not have known what it was because I was so young, but I remember it like it was yesterday. Mom would tell me how I would be sitting in the room with her, and I would point and say," momma there's grandpa." She said I would be pointing and following him with my hand as he was moving. She said I use to scare her so bad. Now that I do not remember. My mom said there were many nights they could hear grandpa's stick coming down the hall. My oldest sister Wilma said he tried to pull the cover from over her head one night. All I know is we have all experienced something or another living on Field Street. I will never forget that house.

CHAPTER

2

SPENDING TIME WITH MOM

Every Saturday morning mom would get us up early and make us clean up the house before getting in the car with her. She always took us on a Saturday outing, and we never knew when we would return. She always took us by Big Mama's house. Big Mama was my biological dad's mother. She always had something for us, even if it was only a hot baked sweet potato. We were always glad to see her. Big Mama was short in statue, and I never knew why we called her big mama instead of grandma. We would leave big mama's and to Uncle Eugene's house that had watermelons. We would be sitting on the benches outside eating watermelon when he would say, "y'all need to leave something for the hogs." I was thinking to myself, how many hogs did Uncle Eugene have. Everybody out there was eating watermelon. Uncle Eugene was my stepdad's uncle. There was a cousin of my stepdad, L.C., that we would sometimes stop to see, but not as much. I never knew what L.C. stood for and I never could remember to ask. We would stop by my grandma's house on my stepdad's side. She had every fruit tree you could name. Her name was Bernice Ross. Her husband's name was Alvin Ross. He was not my stepdad's father. Grandpa Alvin would always ask us how we felt by rubbing our ear lobes. I thought he was a little strange sometimes. We ate fruit until we could not eat anymore. Back then no one washed fruit, we just picked and ate. Sometimes we would rub it on our sleeve before we ate.

But then there was other Saturdays that we would go to the fish bank with mom and stay all day. It was dark when we left and dark when we came back. Mom would stop and get a lot of snacks, fill up the cooler with pops, juice, and water. We had bologna, summer sausages, cheese, and vanilla wafers. I thought the cheese and vanilla wafers was the best; do not drink a Coke with it! We were happy children and we always had plenty to eat. We might not have had everything we wanted to wear, but we had clothes. In our house the clothes were handed down to the younger ones. That was the way it was because it was so many of us. We were a happy and close-knit family. I sometimes wished I had enough money so my mom would not have to work, so she could be with us all the time. Mom worked every day through the week and still managed to have breakfast and dinner ready. Just an amazing woman. We did not know what wearing shoes was when we were at home. We stayed riding our bikes, skating, climbing trees and fences. Everyone thought of Bell and me as tomboys. We did not care; we were having fun. Bell got me in a lot of trouble one day. We were outside playing, and I do not know what happened; but I was calling Bell as she was going in the house, and she would not answer. I called her repeatedly, she still did not answer me. I called her a little black son-of-a-gun, of course, you know it was not 'gun.' What did I say that for, I did not even know what that meant at my age? I knew after I said it it was the wrong thing to say. My stepdad came to the door, my mom was standing behind him. He asked me did I know what I just said. I said, 'yes sir.' He asked me did I know those are bad words. I said no. I could see mom standing behind him laughing so hard. She tried not to let me see her laughing, but I did. My stepdad said you know that daddy is going to whip you for saying that. I said yes sir. I think that was the worst whipping I got from my stepdad. That was an awfully long day for me. After I said those bad words that's when Bell turned around and said, "oh, I am going to tell momma on you." I was so upset with that girl that day until this day, if I am talking to you answer me even if you have to say go jump in a lake. That taught me a lesson. Please do not ignore me again. I never did understand how you can get a whipping for saying something you have no idea or not know the meaning of what you are saying. I did know not to say that again.

Uncle Walter and Aunt Janet came to visit us that weekend. Uncle Walter was my stepdad's brother and Aunt Janet was his wife. They were in walking distance from our house and Aunt Janet needed to go back to her house to get something and as we were walking my mom missed a step and fell. She got up looked at me and said, "please don't tell you daddy I fell." Little did I know that mom was pregnant and lost a baby that same year. I wonder if I had opened my mouth would it have changed things. But I promised her I would not tell my stepdad. I was too young to know at that time what was going on. When I was older, I told mom about it, and she looked at me and said, "Baby you were too young to remember that." She said sometimes I think you have been here before, and I would always laugh when she said things like that.

My oldest brother, Pete, left for Job corps in 1965 and was stationed in Seattle, Washington. He was the first to leave home. Mom was happy that he was trying to do something with his life. Pete was always quiet and kept to himself. He was never the mingling type. No matter what we were having as a family he never stayed long and was always the firs to leave.

I do not know why but he was always considered the black sheep of the family. He never walked with his head up and people would always ask why. I had no answer but one day Pete and I was sitting outside, and I actually got him to talk to me. I asked him if his neck or head ever hurt him? He said he was not bothered with headaches or anything of the sort. I asked again why he held his head down so much and he started talking and I could not believe the things that came out of his mouth. He told me of the year he was in Job Corps he and his Hispanic friend turned over in a truck and he had a brace on his head for about a week during his hospital stay. I was sitting there in disbelief with my mouth wide open. This is the brother that never talks. I asked if mom knew about that accident, and he said yes. That explained a lot just from that one conversation. From that time forward, I never wondered about why he held his head down. Pete is the eldest of the bunch and weighed fifteen pounds when he as born. Mom said he almost killed her. I am sure that a figure of speech. But always said it anyway!

One day as I stood in the front door of the house, a neighbor that lived on the corner down the street from us came dragging his leg with a knife sticking out the calf of his leg and his pant leg split wide open. I heard Ms. Mary, our nosy neighbor, hollering and screaming asking him what happened but he kept walking not saying a word to her. Mom came to the door behind me and when she saw him, she said "Oh Lord." At the same time, Russel my brother, came running to tell mom that Jerry had cut Jimmie. Mom told Russel to go get Jerry and bring him home. When Jerry made it home, he told mom Jimmie kept messing with him and she said why did you have to cut him. It was not intentional, when Jimmie turned and started walking away, I took the knife out of my pocket and threw it at him, I did not know it was going to hit him. Even though I did not mean to hurt him, everyone tried to remain calm. My mom and Jimmie's mom were friends and they talked to each other from time to time, as I said earlier, we were a big happy family on that street. Jerry did get into trouble and one time even went to jail for a while. Mom said he was just mean.

My brother, Jerry, is mom's second eldest son, he enlisted in the Vietnam War. I remember through the neighborhood that day but was too young to understand what was happening. We were all sitting outside as Jerry walked up to the porch and mom asked him where he had been. He replied, "I just enlisted in the Army." Mom yelled, "boy stop playing with me." Jerry said, mom I really did. She asked him who told you you could enlist in a war. He said, nobody, I told myself. Mom cried uncontrollably and I felt so bad for her. Jerry was telling her not to cry that he will be all right. Mom said how do you know you are going to be all right. Jerry said, "mom, I just know." He was always a strong-willed person. Once he made up his mind to do something that was it. Jerry and I were awfully close; I guess it was because we looked so much alike. Not hearing from Jerry for weeks at a time took a toll on mother. When she did receive a letter, it was dated weeks earlier and the worst part was the blood stains on the pages. I remembered how she would cry and cry and sometimes she would not get a letter from him for months. Jerry was the only one of five brothers that went to the army. There were times we would see a black car driving through the neighborhood and felt for sure it was someone from the armed forces coming to tell us he had been killed in service. I do remember one day hearing a lady hollering so loud you could hear her it seemed on the other side of town because she had received the bad news. We all stood around crying for her and with her because it could have been anyone's son or brother. When Jerry did return home from the war it was the happiest day of our lives. Mom was the happiest because she cooked everything he like, and we stayed up with him half the night.

Later as time passed, Jerry started having nightmares. He would wake up yelling, running down the hall and throwing things. Mom would make us go back to bed. It hurt her to see him in that condition. Jerry and I was in a conversation some time later and I asked him about his nightmares at night. What he told me brought tears to my eyes. He told me of the men, women, and children he had to kill in the war comes back to haunt him. He finds himself running after them ; trying to catch them. I asked if he really had to kill children. He said he had to because the enemy would send their own children with bombs strapped to them to blow them up. So, it was me or them. I really hated what the war did to my brother. Jerry later married and moved away. The relationship between the two of them was unpleasant. I hated the way they got along and so did mom although there was nothing; we could do about it. All the pleading and talking we tried to offer them never helped.

In June of 1966, Dr. Martin Luther King, Jr. came to Price, Mississippi. Everyone was so excited; there was hustling and bustling all over the town. Mom and my stepdad put all of us in the back room and told us to be quiet and close the door. That was a scarry time, but mom stayed in the room with us. Soon we started hearing loud noises, people shouting and screaming; the sound was terrifying. When my stepdad rushed back into the house, he said tear gas was being thrown, men were walking on top of buildings, people's eyes were full of tear gas and they had to call in the S.W.A.T. Team from the city of Jackson, Mississippi. That day went down in history, and I will never forget it.

I have been blessed to visit the Ebenezer Baptist Church in Atlanta, Georgia, the house where he grew up, the museum and the place where they fed the homeless. All in memory of Dr. King. The hardest day for the whole nation was the day Dr. King was assassinated in April of 1968 on the balcony outside his second-story room at the Lorraine Motel in Memphis, Tennessee. A young man died at the age of thirty-nine and was buried in his hometown of Atlanta, Georgia. I do remember my mom crying that whole day along with neighbors and the whole nation. It was as if the whole world stood still. There will never be another one like him. He was one of God's truest vessels.

Mom and Aunt Edna would sometimes go out on the town. I remember mom keeping her shoes under her bed. I went under that bed for mom's shoes so many times. I can still hear her calling, "one of y'all come go under this bed and get my shoes." I knew then she and Aunt Edna were getting ready to 'step out.' That was the phrase she always used. Mom was a beautiful lady and really looked good when she dressed up. I never wanted her to go out because I thought she was always supposed to be home with us. But having twelve children at home, she needed a break sometimes! I do not know how she did it. Women back then were made out of much stronger material than we are today.

I used to love listening to mom as she would tell me about the day I was born. She said it was about six inches of snow on the ground, the lights were off, and dad was at another woman's house. She got up and went to the woman's house to get him with bee flappers on her feet in the snow with a young baby at home. If it were not for the people she worked for at the time, she does not know how she would have made it. They made sure we had groceries and the lights stayed on. They helped her until she was able to get back to work. They owned a café in town. Thank you for looking out for my mom! She did not tell me the whole story until years later and when she did, I stayed mad with my biological dad for years.

CHAPTER

FOOD WAS GOOD BACK THEN

I never will forget the man that would come in the neighborhood every
Saturday morning in a truck filled with the biggest buffalo fish I had
ever seen. Everybody in the neighborhood bought those fish. I never
knew if he caught them himself or if he bought them from someone else
to resale. All I know is everybody in the neighborhood ate fish every
weekend. Those that was not able to buy for themselves, other people
shared with them. During the holidays it was the same way. Everyone
cooked and everyone shared. Mom would cook so many cakes and pies
because she knew that she needed enough for us and everybody else.
Every time she cooked it was enough to feed a crowd: dressing, potato
salad turkey, ham, greens and ham hocks, cornbread, macaroni, and
cheese. You name it, we had it. We always had plenty to eat. Mom put
the foods that needed refrigeration in the fridge but there was one thing
that I could never understand how the cakes and pies stayed so fresh.
All mom did was put a white sheet over them on the table. It seemed

the older those cakes and pies were, the better they tasted. Everything tasted better the next day or so. There was always a lot of turkey left. We ate turkey salad, turkey spaghetti, turkey sandwiches, my God, I often wonder when all the turkey will would be gone.

On New Year's day there would never be enough black-eyed peas, cornbread, or fried chicken. There were never any left over after that holiday; of course, we always had a cake or banana pudding or pies.

There were a few desserts that mom cooked all the time blackberry pie, bread pudding, and rice pudding. I tell you that I ate so much of that stuff growing up that I hate it today, especially the blackberry pie. I thought one time mom had a blackberry bush hidden somewhere.

CHAPTER

MOVING INTO OUR NEW HOUSE

Before we moved, my stepdad bought a floor model stereo with the television included. We would watch it sometimes, but he really got it for the new house that was being built. When we were not watching it, they kept it covered up. Back then if you had a television, you were doing good.

We moved into our new house in October of 1968. Everyone was so excited. I thought it was the most beautiful house I had ever seen. We did not see cracks in the floor anymore. We had sidewalks so we could skate and ride our bikes. We were so happy! There was this big glass door that led out to the carport. My older sister, Wilma, walked right into it trying to go out the door. That is how clear the glass was. She paid attention to it from then on. The girls had a room, and the boys had a room. However, no one had their own separate room. We did not care; we were ok with the current arrangement. We did not make many friends with the other children in the neighborhood. I do not know why, I guess we were just being kids. My sister, Bell, did most of the 'picking' back and forth from across the street. My cousin, Sally, was not any better. I was mostly the quiet one but was the one that ended up in a fight with one of the neighbors. Her mom, Anna, and her brother, Bradley, lived next door to the other neighbor that we did not have a good relationship with. The girl's name was Samantha. I never said anything to any of them. However, the day Samantha and I got into a fight I was riding my bike when Samantha and two of her friends were coming pass me on the sidewalk. She pushed up against me and I almost fell. I jumped off the bike and we fought until my brother, Jack, pulled me off of her in a ditch. The other two girls, Tammy, and Christine were also our neighbors along with their brother, Eric, came down the street also behind my brother. They also had another brother, Kevin. I really liked Kevin, but I think his eyes were somewhere else. We all walked back down the street, still going back and forward at each other with words. I was never bothered with any of them again. If you were to ask why I was picked out of the bunch to fight one of the other girls, the only thing I could see would have been I was quiet. The quiet ones usually are the ones to get singled out and picked on. As to this day, I never bother anyone, just do not bother me. Usually, I can have a good relationship with anybody. Mom always taught us not to bother anyone but if they put their hands on us, if we did not whip them, she was going to whip us. Hey, I would rather whip them than for mom to whip me.

My Aunt Terry, on my stepdad's side of the family was a big woman, but she was also attractive. She had a husband, Leroy, who really loved her. She did not want for anything. Mom said they had been married for a long time. Aunt Terry's son, Riley, was killed over a two-dollar pool game downtown Price we called the 'hollow' Aunt Terry never got over his death and could hardly talk about it. Riley had also been in the war at one time. I did not spend a lot of time around this family. They did come to visit us, but I do not know if my mom or stepdad ever visited them.

Aunt Terry had another son, Willie. Willie was very outspoken. I mean he did not care what he said. It was something about him, although I never felt comfortable around him. I found out later in life why. He told me that he had asked my stepdad for me when I was a little girl. I could not believe my ears. I just knew that he was just talking because he really was not kin to me by blood. But I always felt if you were in the family that you were family. No if, and, or buts about it, that is how I saw it. When Willie looked at me and said, Really, I asked Jed for you, and he told me that I was crazy that you was his baby." I knew then that he was telling me the truth because that is something my stepdad would have said. Why was he telling me this now? I always knew there was something I could not put my finger on, but I would have never guessed that. All I knew he catered to me all the time. So, that is why all the attention I received from him came from. Wow! Just unbelievable, Lord what is next? Aunt Terry died of cancer. It was a great loss for the family. Aunt Terry was my step grandma's only daughter. My sister, Millie, looked just like her. She could have been mistaken for her daughter. I can recall times when Millie would tell me how her son, Willie, would stare at her telling her how much she looked like Aunt Terry.

Saturday mornings remained the same. Mom's car just got smaller and smaller the older we got. At one time it looked like no one was going to leave home. My brothers, Pete, and Jerry got married but everyone else remained home. About a year later, my brother, Jack, went to live with my biological dad after his wife died. I always thought she was mean. We called her, Robin. Before we could walk in the door, she would say, "your daddy ain't got no money." My sister Bell and I would just look at each other. Why did she always think that we just came to see daddy just to get money from him. Jack and daddy got along good. Jack looked a lot like daddy. Daddy always wanted me to pull all of his eye lashes out. He said they got in his eyes, but I could not see that. His eye lashes were already very scarce, but I would sit and pull every little hair I saw. He was the first person I have ever known to do that. I am my daddy's baby. I never had a chance to spend a lot of time with my daddy. Daddy was a heavy drinker and smoker. Mom said it was part of the reason she could not stay with him. My stepdad raised me from six months old. I thought he was the tallest and biggest man I had ever seen.

My brother Russel, who was the third oldest boy, got married. His wife and him fought all the time though. She threw a peanut butter jar at him and almost cut his ear off. I remember that day when he came around to the back yard holding his ear. There was so much blood. Mom took him to the hospital and got it sewed back on. But that did not stop the violence. The next weekend they were right back into it all over again. Russel's wife name was Raven. My brother Jerry and Raven had a misunderstanding and Russel wanted to beat him up. That was something we never did was to fight each other. Mom kept saying something was wrong with Russel and he needed help. The next thing I knew, Russel's wife, Raven, had gotten on a train and left Mississippi. All I was told was that if she wanted to live, she had to leave him. They had two sons together. I was told Russel was a good dancer and the ladies loved dancing with him. He always had jokes and was the life of the party. Girls were always flirting with him. Russel had been married two times before. He and his second wife was not together long. I never knew what happened. She was a good person and was easy to get along with. His last wife is a jewel. She has always remained the same.

One Sunday morning, mom left for church. She told us not to get the bikes out the storage room that day. My sister Bell waited until mom left and got the bikes out anyway. Do you remember me telling you how Bell always got me in trouble? Well, this is one of those days mom usually locked the storage room door. Bell tells me to get on the handlebar of her bike and she would ride down the street. As we were riding Bell hit a big rock and it threw me off the bike. I was hollering so Mrs. Reese Eldridge took me to the emergency room. Bell kept telling me not to cry. When mom got to the hospital, she did not say a word. When mom did not talk it was time to be worried. On the way home she still did not say a word. I was praying all the way home. I dared not to say anything. I had a cast on my left leg and Bell only had a scratch on her arm. I still have that scar on my leg. When everybody was settled down in the house that is when mom said something. I will never forget those words. She said to me, "didn't I tell you all not to get those bikes out of the storage room." I said, 'yes ma'am.' I just knew whenever I got out of that cast and crutches, I was going to get a whipping, but I never did.

Mom had a big heart, and she would open her doors to anyone who needed somewhere to stay. Once mom allowed her stepdad, his wife, and children to live with us. However, they only stayed a couple of months. We all got along good. That was the kind of woman she was although she did not take any mess. It was a different situation when my cousins who lived next door came to live with us for a while. For some reason, we did not get along at all. That may have been because we never have been that close to each other under one roof. But by the grace of God, we got through it. After that, mom said she did not think she would ever let anyone else live with us again.

Our stepdad was always on us about sitting on the back of his car. We were not like the kids today, we loved being outdoors. My brother, Walter, was always reminding us he did not want us sitting on the car. Of course, we did not listen to him. So, on this particular day, after telling my sister Clara to get off the car, he grabs her by the legs and pulls her off the car. We had a concrete driveway and Clara hit her forehead. She looked so abnormal I just knew Walter had cracked her skull. My stepdad told mom that he could not whip him because he told Walter to keep them off the car. Walter was sorry for what he had done, and I could see it all over his face. It seemed like it took forever for that knot to go down on Clara's forehead. What was always funny to me was that when the accident happened mom called every daughter's name she had until she finally said, 'girl you know who I am talking to" so she could take care of her. She never called the name she was trying to call. Believe me I did understand. Having twelve children, she had that right. Mom told us stories about how women back then would have a baby one day and the next day they would be back in the field picking cotton. She said sometimes it would be the same day. Tell me if you know of a lady today who can do that. I know I can not think of anyone.

I tell you that Walter was always getting into something. Mom had gone to work on this day when he decided he was going to take my sister Wilma's friend, Gary, to the hospital. Mom had ridden to work with some co-workers that day. I never will forget that car. It was a Pontiac with a brown top and the body was yellow. I do not know what year model it was. But when mom got home and saw her car, she put her hands on her hips and asked, "What happened to her blank-blank car?" I dare not say what mom really said. We were so quiet for a minute, then everyone started talking at one time. She told everyone to hush because she could not hear everyone at the same time. Mom got somebody to come over and repair the pole that Walter had hit with the car. She did not want the corner of the house to fall down. As upset as she was, she was more concerned about how Gary was doing.

My stepdad had a friend, Mr. Damien, and the two of them went out all times of the day and night. Mr. Damien looked scarry to me. They went out with a metal piece that helped them locate money. I asked my stepdad how it worked, and he told me it was a magnet and sometimes he would say it was a detector. It helped him and Mr. Damien find hidden treasures. The magnet on the end of it would show them exactly where the money was. Mr. Damien wore black suits and hats all the time, plus he was a very dark skinned himself. That is why I think I was so afraid of him. He reminded me of a vampire. But he and my stepdad got along well. I had been told that all kinds of spirits hung around buried treasures and we have experienced some strange things happening in this house. My sister Stella said she saw a lady standing over by the stove one night. We thought she was just trying to scare us. I started to believe she did see something after I experienced a shadow of a ball-headed man standing outside the bedroom window. There was a storm that night and all the lights were out. Mom told me that when you look for something, you see something. So, I let that one go, but never forgot it. But okay, explain this to me. I was sitting outside on the front porch one evening, just knowing that my brother Walter was in the house. Mom had left and took everybody with her but Walter and I, so I thought. The phone start ringing, you know we had phones on the wall back then. I opened the door to the house and shouted to Walter to please answer the phone because it kept ringing. Walter walks out the door, never looking at me slamming the door behind him and asked me "why can't you answer the phone? I told him, you are in the house, you could answer it. Walter turns and goes back in the house. I jump up going behind him just fussing, all the way to the back yard in the dark by myself. So, I gave up and said" I am not playing games with you." I thought Walter was hiding from me. I sat back down on the porch.

About twenty or thirty minutes later mom pulls up on the driveway and Walter got out of the back seat. My mouth dropped to the floor; I could not speak for a minute. My first thought was they were playing a game on me. So, I asked mom did Walter leave with her. She looks at me and said yes girl. I said mom he could not have because Walter had just come to the door a while ago talking to me. Mom sat down and asked me what was I talking about, are you crazy? I told mom what happened to me, and she said if that happened to you baby you need to pray. Mom would always listen to me when I told here something. It took me a long time to get over that. When I say some unexplained things has happened, believe me it is true. Who in this world could ever explain that to me and make me understand?

When I did meet someone else, he lied about having a girlfriend. Bell met her boyfriend Quincy first, Quincy had a friend named Lionel, he wanted me to meet. He lied and said he didn't have anyone in his life. Everything was going fine until one day we were outside in the driveway and this car stops and two ladies jumped out of the car. One of them cut Quincy and the other one slapped Lionel. It was a mess, and my mom was in the house. I was trying to quiet things down before she came to the door. I had never experienced so much violence in my life. I told Lionel that is what happens when you lie about things. I never could understand why a grown person feel like they have to lie. That was a relationship that never began, thank God it did not. I am a quiet person and live a quiet life.

I made a huge mistake in the next relationship. I am not proud of it today, but back then I said it was okay. Today, looking back it was a very dumb thing to do. He was a nice man but did not care what time of day he came in that driveway. May I add, I am still at home with mom, and she blew up at me when she saw him standing at the door one day. He acted as if he was not married. I would ask him not to come to the house so much. He would always say ok but did the opposite. I knew that something had to change with him, or we were going to have a disaster. His name was Stanley. This man got to the point where he wanted me stuck up under him all the time. On Valentine's Day he pulls up on the driveway and have a big teddy bear and the biggest box of candy hanging out of the window waiting on me to come out to get it. During Valentine's Day then everybody would be sitting out being nosy trying to see who was going to get a delivery. You can imagine how I felt. I just knew this was not going to end well because Price was a small town, and everybody knew everybody. I knew I had to break it off with him. So, I started talking to him about not seeing so much of each other and he did not want to hear that. So, I started seeing someone else. I knew for sure this would do it. While having company one night, he came over and showed out trying to make me get in the car and leave with him. He talked bad about the guy that I had invited over saying things like did I know what kind of guy he was; that he was the worst guy around town; his name was Drake. People was standing out looking and whispering. I asked him not to do this in my mom's driveway. It was the worst day ever; I just could not understand this man acting like he was not married. It took me three months to get this man to leave me alone. I heard that he started dating a girl around the corner from me. I did not care who he was dating as long as it was not me. I realized later that you do so much damage when you go inside of a woman's home. When you learn better, you do better. Of course, he continued to do what he was doing. I was young and innocent, really, I was. I was still in high school.

CHAPTER

MY DREAMS

As time passed, I became a dreamer. I guess that is what I have always been. In my teen years, I started having dreams. About two weeks before a tornado came through and ripped our town away, I would dream about tornadoes nearly every night. I would tell my mom about them. I can remember dreaming the exact same dream. I dreamt I was here in the house and could hear thunder and the wind blowing so hard. I was not in this house, I do not know whose house I was in but every door I went to trying to get out a tornado was headed straight at me. I just remembered standing in the middle of that floor just screaming to the top of my voice. As I was screaming, I was turning around and around, at that moment I would awaken from my dream. Mom told people how I had been having these dreams about a tornado as I was going through some thing at that time and was too young to understand.

The next dream was about a plane crash. This plane always landed on the back of Ms. Eldridge's house who lived across the street from us. I would dream that dream over and over again. I told mom about that dream as well. She said I hope that nothing bad was going to happen. So, on this day I was sitting on the couch watching TV and there was breaking news of an airplane crash. My first thought was why are they telling this old news. Then it hit me that I had been dreaming about this airplane crash earlier. That was the crash where the most people in the history of the United States had died. As I looked back on that airplane crash it was on May 25th 1979, and 258 passengers and crew was on board along with 2 people on the ground. It was a flight going from Chicago to Los Angeles, California. Once again, my mouth dropped. When I called mom, I was in a hissy as my big momma would say. Mom looked at what was going on the TV and said," you are just a different child from any of my other children." She also told me that God was doing a great work in me. It might seem strange to a lot of you, but I have had many dreams that has come true. Some of my dreams if I told you, you would never believe. It used to scare me when I was young because I did not understand them. But it does not bother me now because I have grown in Christ. My spirit has gotten calmer now. I am a dreamer and I have come to accept that.

Going back to the tornado that tore Price to pieces, we were without lights and gas for weeks. Those were the days we really appreciated Bologna sandwiches, Viennas, crackers, cheese, cookies, hog-head sauce, and pork-n-beans. We were so blessed to have a house still standing and in one piece. Some people had nothing, having to sleep in the school gym or wherever they could. For some reason that day we did not know where mom was, but later found out she was in Meshan working. Mom told us how the police officer would not let her come through the barricades. But when she explained to the officer that she had twelve children in Price, he allowed her to go through but told her to be very careful. Mom said she was going to get through even if she had to walk; that is how mom was.

There were houses sitting upside ways in the ditch, houses that had been lifted completely off the foundation, nothing left but the floor. We were all in school when the tornado hit. My stepdad came to get us in his work van. I never will forget that day; every cloud in the sky was in front of the sun. It was so dark, the scariest day of my life. Everybody was helping each other by opening their doors to those that needed help, giving clothes and food. One thing I can say about Price, we would look out for each other in a time of need. We stayed out of school for weeks. March 29, 1976 will never be forgotten. We missed mom's cooking doing that time, which let us know how much you appreciate something when you do not have it anymore. We did some kind of eating when the lights and gas was back on. Mom taught us all to cook. I was cooking a full meal by the time I was twelve. I learned everything but the baking, but I can do enough to get by. My brothers can cook also.

I started working at a little store downtown. Mr. and Mrs. Howard owned the store. I enjoyed working there but did not like dipping ice cream. That was the hardest ice cream to dip. I worked there for a couple of years. My sisters Wilma and Stella worked around the corner at another business in the middle of town. The Mason's ran this business. Out of the seven girls, three of us worked there including me. There were three brothers, a niece, and a nephew. The three brothers were Reese Mason, Jeff Mason and Benjamin Mason. The nephew was Parker Mason and the niece was Lois Mason. They had three other people that worked there that was of no relation to them. Their names were Marvin Long, Dora Parker and Harry Miller. They were all very nice people. I really liked working with them. My mom and Ms. Lois Mason became friends over the years. Ms. Lois was always complaining and talking about how her day was going. I thought she was bad company because she would always ask one of us to walk down the street to the store to get her a Goody powder and a RC cola. She was a sweet person; she was just so negative. I know that later on my mom started taking BCs with a Dr. Pepper. My sister Bell and I started working at the chicken poultry in a near by town. We worked there every summer so we could buy our clothes for school. We were the two mom did not have to worry about. We thought we were some of the best dressed girls in the class. It was night when we went to work and dark when we got home. We road on a bus that went that route every day. Mom always told people that Bell and I were good girls, and she never had any trouble with us. We would sometimes go to the movie downtown. When we left the movies, we would go looking for our brothers. We did not care where they went, we were right behind them. Jerry would tell mom, "Mom make those girls stay at home." We said we were going to play pool one night when we left the movie, this was on a Saturday might. Our brothers had taught us to play, and we loved playing the game. These men started picking at us saying things like, "let us guys have the table, y'all don't know how to play." I had a fifth of wine on the table and so did Bell. Bell said to me, "if they keep bothering us, we are going to hit them in the head with our bottles." I said, Oh Lord, please let them go on because I knew Bell would do it if I did not. The Lord must have heard my prayer because when we looked around, we saw my stepdad walk through the door along with Jerry and Russel, my two brothers. I do not know if someone told them we were there, or it was just a coincident that they walked in. Nevertheless, they came over to the table and asked Bell and I what we were doing, and we explained to them what was going on. One of the men started talking to my stepdad. The man asked him did he know us, and he said, "these are my daughters." He began shaking my stepdad's hand telling him he did know that we were his daughters. They can play as long as they want. Bell and I looked at each other and played one more game and let the men have the table. We left and followed my brothers across the street to a café that my brother liked, Jerry was always in there. If you wanted to find him, go to Tier Café. This night, he left and went to another café. Later, I went around the corner to where he was to Daisy's Hideaway. He was sitting at the table with some other people, he did not see me right away. I looked on the table where they were sitting and there was a long line of BC Powder on the table. Jerry looked up and saw me, he was so angry. He had never gotten angry with me like that before. He hollered at me asking me what I was doing there. Get out of here! I left and went back to Tier Café where Bell was. Jerry later apologized to me because he knew I was upset. He said there are some things you just do not need to see. At that time, I still did not know what I saw and for years I wondered what all that powder was doing on the table. I know now what it was and if I had known then I probably would have told mom. The reason I would have told is because that was a bad thing and I always told her about things that was not right.

One day Bell and I was walking across the track when these two guys in a car started talking to us. They asked if we wanted a ride, of course, you know what the answer was. Their names were Scott and Mark. Scott was the one I ended up talking to and Bell ended up talking to Mark. Scott was my first boyfriend, and he was four years older than I was. I never knew how old Mark was, I did not want to be nosy. Scott and I got along good; his older sister Diane did not like me for some reason. His mom, Ms. Violet, and his two younger sisters, Louise and Sadie, seem to like me. We would sometimes go out to the Reservoir to picnic and get in the water. Scott could swim and so could Mark. I would not let Scott take me out too far in the water. Scott worked at the chicken poultry where Bell and I worked during the summer. Scott had another friend named Stanley. Stanley and Scott started hanging together pretty close. One night we were down to my uncle Shelby's café, Uncle Shelby was my mom's brother, and he was always in business doing something, when I noticed that I had not seen Scott for a minute. I went outside looking for him when Stanley, his friend, asked me who was I looking for. I said I was looking for Scott and have you seen him? Stanley said, 'no' and he began to help me look for him. My sister, Wilma, lived up above Uncle Shelby's café, so I went up there looking for him but still did not see him. When I came back down, Stanley said, "let's ride up the street and see if we see him." Like my mom always told me; I was wise beyond my years. So, we get to this apartment complex, Stanley pulls up in the parking lot and flashed his lights. I'm saying to myself, I was not supposed to have noticed that, really! So, we go back down the street to my uncle's café, guess who comes up riding a bike by the time we got out of the car. I asked Scott where he went, he was looking across the field somewhere just lying. He could not even look me in my face. I listened to him talk for a minute. I said to him, okay. You have said the same thing twice. So as time went on things come out, which it usually does. We were out at a club one night and as we start to the dance floor this girl comes up grab him by the collar and said, "You are dancing with me this time." He stood there with both of his hands up. Scott stood about six feet tall. He is looking at me all the time saying, "I don't know what is going on, I promise you I don't." So, me being me, went back to the table got my things and was getting ready to leave. Bell and Mark was at the club that night as well. Bell wanted to jump on her, but I told her that Scott knew what was going on. I was on my way out the door when he came behind me telling me that he worked with this girl at the chicken poultry. He claimed he did not know why she did that. Oh, he swore to the last that he was innocent. Now, you know what my next questions was. I asked him where does this girl live? When he called the name of the street, that is the same street that his friend, Stanley, turned on at the apartment complex when he flashed the lights that night. He was at her house that night. I just knew he was going to lie, but I asked him had he ever been to her house? The answer was no. I told him that I knew he wasn't telling me the truth. Like I said he was my first boyfriend, that situation did hurt me.

I forgave Scott, but I never forgot it. How can I trust a man that don't do anything but lie? We dated until he moved to Maryland. I knew in my heart that this was going to be the end of our relationship. When he got stationed in Maryland, he wanted me to come visit, but you know mom did not want me to go. Mom said I was too young, but you have the mind of a twenty or twenty-five year old, so she let me go. Mom and Scott had a long conversation on the phone that night. I don't know what they talked about because she asked me to leave the room. I had a good time when I made it to Maryland, we were always on the go. He showed me all the attractions and beaches; it was awesome. After I made it back home, he called mom and asked her if I could come to stay. The answer was no, of course. He promised her that he would make sure I finished school. The answer was still no. She told him that she had already did something against her principles for letting me come to visit him in the first place. I knew that this surely was the end of our relationship. Scott called me a lot at first, then the calls became less and less. The next time I saw Scott, he had come home to tell me that he was engaged to be married. He did not have a good approach. When we were alone that day, he held his hand up and said do you see this, with his ring finger sticking out. I said, yes, I see it, that's a nice ring. I congratulated him and also told him it is never what you do but how you do it. It was hard, but I kept it moving. About a year later, I ran into him in TJ Maxx with a young lady he said was his wife's daughter. He asked me why I was looking at him like that, that he was old enough to be her daddy. I guess she was maybe between ten and twelve. I did not see him again until one day he dropped by my sister Wilma's house. We were all playing cards when he came up. He stayed for a few minutes, then took off. The only thing he asked or said to me was how was I doing. I wonder if he ever looked back on that day that he rudely told me he was engaged.

If it was meant for us to be together, we would be together today. God does not make any mistakes. I really wished them all the happiness. I have always wanted him to be happy. I think that is why I started being drawn to older men ever since; I don't know, I just wonder about it. I did not date for a long time after that relationship.

CHAPTER

6

MY HIGH SCHOOL YEARS

Finishing high school was the goal now. I needed to concentrate on that now. It seemed like the school year was going so slow. I ended up in a teacher's room that my sister Bell had, a couple of years later. Bell and Mrs. Pierce did not get along; they got into it. Bell ended up with a long scratch on her arm. Mom asked Bell what happened. She told mom that Mrs. Pierce scratched her arm with a ruler that she was trying to snatch out of her hand. Mom went to the school the next day to talk to Mrs. Pierce. They kept calling her over the intercom, but she would not come. So, the principal Mr. Brown, went to get her. When Mrs. Pierce came in the door mom jumps at her trying to grab her. Principal Brown came between them and took mom out of the office. He told mom that she scared Mrs. Pierce to death. He begged her to leave and promised her that she would never have to come back to the school. He promised her that what ever happened he would take care of it. Lord, I was so glad that mom did not get her hands on this lady! So, as

I walked through Mrs. Pierce's door, she look at me and asked, 'you are Bell Wilson's sister, aren't you?' I said yes, I am. She turned up her nose at me. I dare not say anything to mom about me being in her room. I knew what mom's reaction would be. Mrs. Pierce was so hard on me; I did not get that fourth of unit from her either. I ended up getting it my senior year in school It was so embarrassing having to take ninth grade state government as a senior, but I had to have it to graduate.

Mr. Pruitt was another teacher that for some reason we did not get along with at all. Everyday I walked into his room he always had something to say. One thing he would ask me was did I have everything I needed for his class. He would say do not ask to be excused to go back to get anything. I would not say anything to him when he would ask me that; it was my senior year and I wanted everything to run smoothly.

This particular day I don't know what was going on, but he snapped at me because I was looking on the book with my best friend, Tracey. He asked me where is your book, Wilson? I told him I was running late and did not get a chance to get it. He goes on to say, 'you think you gone walk that line don't you Wilson?" I looked at him and said to him, "If I don't walk that line no one will walk." What did I say that for, Mr. Pruitt told me to get out my room Wilson and do not come back unless you have your parents with you? I could not believe this man, he started with me first. I knew I should not have said what I said because my mom taught me better than that. Mom told us no matter what, always respect your elders. I left the room not knowing what to do. My stepdad worked for the school system in maintenance, I went to see if I could find him to come down to talk to Mr. Pruitt. Of course, my stepdad asked me what I did, and I told him. He looks at me and said, 'now you know better than that." I told him that I was sorry that I knew I was wrong, but Mr. Pruitt started in on me first. My stepdad went down to the room with me. When we walked in my stepdad and Mr. Pruitt walks over to the door. Mr. Pruitt shook my stepdad's hand and said I didn't know that she was your daughter. Mr. Pruitt asked me to sit down. They finished talking and my stepdad left. Lord, all I could think of is what is going to happen when I get home. Mom did say to me that she taught me better than that. I said I know mom, I am sorry. My friend Tracey said to me the next day that she did not think I did anything wrong, and Mr. Pruitt needed to stop picking on people. Tracey, Purvis and I were best friends. We looked out for each other. Purvis was Tracey's boyfriend. I wondered what was going to be next. There was always an eventful day at Price High School.

Mr. Mason was a teacher that kept me laughing. I loved going to his room. Mr. Mason was one of the brothers that drove a cab. Every student in the room came to the conclusion that he had to be allergic to deodorant because he was always scratching under his arm. When he talked, he would spit on you, and he had an unpleasant breath. I never understood how he would come in your face talking knowing he was spitting because he always wiped his mouth. He would say things to make everybody laugh. I asked him one day if I could go to my locker to get my tablet. He said no Wilson, you will get it in May. Everybody started laughing at what he said so he starts to laugh. He did let me go after everybody quieted down. Sometimes he would tell us a joke and he would be the only one laughing; then we would laugh at him. Everybody loved Mr. Mason.

Mr. Pedro was another teacher that all the kids loved. I think he was much funnier than Mr. Mason to me. There was something he would say sometimes that I did not like to hear and that was "I got mine, you got to get yours." We as students heard that from most of our teachers. Other than that, he kept us laughing and don't let someone come in the room with something new on. He would call them to the front and ask everyone to look at how good they looked. He asked a student about his new shoes one day; come on up to the front of the room. When he got to the front of the room, he asked him to turn around telling him how good his shoes looked. Then he would ask him where he got his shoes from. After he would tell him, Mr. Pedro would holler out Fred Dollar special! Everybody would fall out laughing. He was one of the best English teachers ever. There were days when we would come in the room and Mr. Pedro would say "okay class we are going to have an oral pop quiz." He would go down the roll in alphabetical order and ask a question. He would say 'going, going, gone, you get an F." Mr. Pedro was really writing something down in the grade book and he never said anything else about it. I just didn't know what to make of him on these days at all. My classmates and myself were upset and quiet on those days. Other than that, he was an awesome teacher in spite of.

Mr. Robinson was our Driver's Education teacher, and he was funny too. He took us out driving down the Natchez Trace and everywhere. We would already be nervous when one of us was under the wheel. He would say things like 'there is a stop sign there are you going to stop?' Or he would say something like, 'what color is that red light?' just anything to make us laugh. He was very laid-back. I think that is why all the students like him. We were riding one day and the student that was driving would holler, whoa! Whoa! On Awards Day, he gave him an award for the worse driver. He told the whole gym that day what he said, and he didn't know what was going on with him. I guess he thought he was plowing a mule. He had everybody in the gym laughing. It was never a dull moment around Mr. Robinson.

Mrs. Jennings was my Algebra teacher. She was such a quiet person and I never heard her get loud. She would always stand at her door as you entered her room. I was like most kids, wondering where in life will I need to know this kind of math. So as time went on, I did what I had to do in her class but that was one class I did not like at all. I voiced to her one time how I struggled to keep my grades up. Mrs. Jennings would say to me that if you want to get it, you will. If you don't get it now, you will see it your first year in college. I said I know you know Mrs. Jennings because you have gone through college already. So, I went to my seat and like I said; did what I needed to do to pass her class. My first year in college when I looked at my schedule, you know what the first subject on there was, Algebra. I saw Mrs. Jenning's face when she was telling me you will see it again. The only thing I would say was, get ready! Mrs. Jennings later passed away. She was a great Math teacher. The school district at Price High School named a building after her. Mrs. Jennings was a great math teacher and had a great impact on many students lives as well as the faculty and friends.

Mr. Johnson was another teacher that taught Math. He was pretty cool, but he wanted you to get that Math. He didn't talk much at all. Mr. Johnson and I always recognized each other sometimes with a hug. We did not think anything of the way we greeted each other, but there were some that did. He said to me one day that we needed to stop greeting each other like we had been because people were getting upset about it. We both laughed about it and for that moment on it was "Hello, how are you doing?" We remained friends over the years. I knew Mr. Johnson would never tell me who it was because he was a peaceful man. I never asked him who it was. Today there is a school named after him. He's no longer with us; he has another home now. God wants some good soldiers too. Mr. Johnson you are truly missed.

Mrs. Walker was and still is a very classy lady. We loved this teacher too. She is an awesome lady. I have never seen a lady that could type so fast. I mean sometimes I thought to myself that her fingers had to be sore. Sometimes I would just sit and watch her type. I tried to get up to a hundred words a minute but never did. She was a still is a very classy lady; very down to earth. One day my best friend didn't come to class, and she asked me, "where is Tracey today, Wilson?" I told her I don't know. Mrs. Walker she then says, 'Oh yes you do." I just couldn't stop laughing at her that day. I really didn't know where she was even though Tracey was always skipping somebody's class. The only thing she told me was that she was not going to typing class that day. I didn't ask her any questions and she didn't volunteer to tell me anything else.

Ms. Sullivan was our school office manager. She was the heart of the school; she knew her stuff. Price Hight School could not have run without her, and everybody knew it. Everybody loved Ms. Sullivan. She kept everybody straight. We would go to her with our problems that we faced on a daily basis. She always told us what we needed to do and that is what we did. In my opinion, she was who ran Price High School. She knew all the students by name and was like a mother figure. She has since retired but is still the same sweet person every time you see her. She is one that deserves much recognition for a job well done. "We love you, Ms. Sullivan!"

About two weeks before graduation, I was going through the lunch line and one of the girls behind me didn't get a box of milk on her tray. Her name was Sherell. All she had to do was walk around the corner to get one. But instead, she says to me real nasty, 'you're going to give me a box of that milk." I said to her that she could ask me better than that Sherell, so since you can't, I'm not going to give you anything. She then say, 'oh, yes you are, you are going to give me a box of that milk"

I then tell her to take it if you're bad. I went on to my seat getting ready to eat. Some of the classmates was urging her on, as well as some of my classmates. As I was sitting there, she came over to my table standing over me. She said, 'give me a box of that milk.' I looked at her and asked her to get away from me. We had red beans that day and they were smoking hot. As I was getting ready to get up and dump the tray on her my Driver Education teacher, Mr. Robinson was standing there. He said to me, 'don't do it Wilson you only have two weeks before graduation.' He said you don't want to get expelled; you're getting ready to graduate. I was so angry and didn't think about that, so I sit down. I thank God for Mr. Robinson that day. She turns and go back to her table. Things were very heated between the two of us that day. She knew that under different circumstances I would have done it. I always walked pass her house on my way home from school. This girl is standing out at the street with a classmate that was her best friend whose name was Francine. I just kept walking not saying anything to her. My mom taught me not to bother anybody, but if they bother me to defend myself. Mom told me that if she ever heard tell of someone whipping my butt that when I got home, she was going to whip me. The next day Sherell came to me and apologized to me. She said, 'I'm sorry about yesterday there is so much going on in my life right now." She said she didn't mean to take it out on me. I told her that I was sorry to hear that, that I hope everything will work out for her. Sherell was a good person in her own way. We all have some ways that we are not proud of. Everyone liked her that's why I was surprised at her reaction over a box of milk.

This one boy in my class asked me if I was all right, his name is Perez. Perez liked me but I didn't like him. Sometimes I would chat with him for a minute; he was just so childish and played a lot. He was very handsome, just not my type. I liked older mature guys. I think that's why I ended up going to my Junior Prom with a guy that had already graduated. My Junior prom was so boring, I made sure I didn't go my Senior year. There was this other classmate whose name was Snyder he liked me too. He was a nice guy I just didn't like him either. Most girls know right off if they like a guy.

I enrolled in Marsh Junior College in the fall. Marsh Junior College was in Marsh County about thirty minutes from Price. I did not have a car, so I rode with some other students. On some days my sister or my mom would take me. I was not sure of what I wanted to major in, so I ended up taking courses like Psychology, Computer Science, Biology, just different courses. On the days I wasn't in class, I substituted at Price High School. It is strange how things happen. I am back subbing at same high school I graduated from. Ms. Sullivan always called me very faithful on those days. It was a good job, it just felt so strange being back at Price High and not as a student. I was in a meeting in the teacher's lounge with them it was amazing. After leaving Marsh Junior college I continued to work at Price High School. I continued to work at Price High School. I think it was a year later when I left. Within the next six months I was engaged.

CHAPTER

MARRYING DRAKE

I met Drake at my sister Millie's house one Saturday night. Drake was eleven years older than I was, so you know he was wiser and smarter. When I met him, I was in a relationship with a married man. The married man I told you about earlier. Drake was one of the ways I got away from him. Drake was friend with my sister's husband, Leo. The first day I met Drake, he told me he was going to be my husband. I looked at him like he was crazy; wondering what kind of man he was. He was drunk I said to myself he didn't know what he was saying. Well, we got closer as time went on Drake bought rings and asked me to marry him and I said yes. My stepdad was furious about it when he heard. At this time, my mom and stepdad was separated. He asked me did I know what I was doing? My answer was, yes sir, I think so. My stepdad said, "no you don't, baby." He said that is not the kind of man you want to marry. He was one of the worst men in town. My brothers felt the same way, but I still married him. No one came to the wedding,

I mean no one! The only people there was his pastor and a few other people I didn't know. I don't know if anyone believed us or not. I have always told myself that I never asked any of them. Drake never told me, but I am sure my stepdad and brothers talked to him.

We moved in a house on Marble Street. At first, everything was going okay. Then I started seeing another side to him. He drank beer, whiskey or whatever all the time. He kept promising me that he was going to quit but he never did. The going out every weekend just wasn't me. I tried to make him understand that. He would say things like, "you act like you are ashamed of me!" I told him he knew better than that. So, he went out every weekend sometimes not making it back home. When I would ask him where he had been, the answer was always at my mom's house. His mom's name was Avery. She was a big influence on Drake; he did listen to her. Drake was working but his mother wanted him to work with some of his friend in St. Louis. I loved Drake's mother and she was a good person. The thing that got to me about Drake was the fact that when he got drunk, he couldn't remember anything; so, he says. He woke up after a drunken night and asked me, "where are my shoes?" I asked him how I would know, you walked in the house with no shoes on. He put on another pair of shoes and said I have to back-track myself to see where I left them. I could not believe what was happening, was this real life? About a half hour later there was a knock on the door. I opened the door and this man asked me, "Do Drake live here?" I told him, yes, and he passed me Drake's shoes and his suit coat. He said I work at Chester Café, and I was watching Drake when he walked in. He ordered a quart of beer, took off his jacket, kicked off his shoes, poured him a cup of beer, took a swallow and he got up and walked out the door. All I could say to this man was, thank you. I sat down on my recliner and asked myself what had I gotten myself into? Did I marry this man too soon or what?

About a month later Drake left for St. Louis to work with his friends. He got out there in St. Louis and forgot he had a wife back home. I found out I was pregnant and everything at that moment looked very dim. I was under a lot of stress during that time. I wasn't working and Drake wasn't sending any money home. I had a miscarriage behind all of that. I tried to hang in there with Drake, but he made it so hard.

Months went by and I met a friend guy whom I could talk with and tell my problems to. Nothing was going on; we were just friends. His name was Pablo. I got a call from Drake telling me that he heard that I was courting on him. He said that he had talked to some of his family members and that is how he knew. I asked him how you could have the nerves to call me to ask about a man when you act like you don't have a wife. I told him he never sent money anymore and he didn't come home like he use too. He got so angry at me, he hung up the phone. That was ok, I was angry too. I guess it was about a month later when I got Drake's tax check in the mail. I cashed it and paid the rent up and bought groceries. I also bought clothes that was long overdue. When he came home looking for the check, I told him I had not seen a check. Drake tracked that check down and he brought a copy of the check over to my mom's house that day. I was visiting mom that day and my sister, Wilma, was also visiting. Drake had a copy of the check and said to me that I know you signed this check, He was on his way back to St. Louis. Wilma said to let her see the check because she knew my handwriting. Wilma looks at the check, looks at me and drops her head. After Drake left, Wilma said you cashed that check, didn't you? I told Wilma how he wasn't sending money home and the bills had piled up. Wilma said, say no more, I see now. She asked me how long he had been doing that and I told her too long. Things really got bad with Drake after that. He got back to St. Louis and did not call or send any money and the bills were getting behind again. So, I decided that I was going to end up going back home to my mom's house.

I left going to the store one Saturday morning and by the time I got in the house, I hear a car horn blow. It was Drake with the guys he ride with. I am standing in the window by this time when Drake gets out of the car and knocks on the door. I wouldn't let him in, so he gets back in the car with his friends and leaves. I don't know where he went and didn't really care. I had a cousin that lived across the street. She was an old lady that was kin to my mom. She called me over and told me that I needed to pack a few clothes and leave. Her name was cousin, Cleo. She said that she had been watching and she thinks he will be back, and it might not be nice. I went back across the street to my house and start packing some clothes. Before I could finish packing, Drake knocks on

the door. I yelled and said, "I'm not going to open the door, Drake!"
By that time, the whole door came down on me. The door knocked me
up against the recliner and I fell on my back. By this time, Drake was
swinging at me, and he was so drunk he could hardly stand up. He was
trying to hit me in my face; since he could not get to my face, he just
beat my legs as I was screaming and kicking. He soon collapsed on the
floor. I got up off the floor hardly able to walk and went to his mom's
house to get them to come get him up off the floor. I told her what had
happened, and she was so upset. I told her that I didn't want him there
with me anymore. She then got his two sisters to come with her to get
him off the floor. His sisters' names were Madelyn, Nora, and Hailey.
Hailey wasn't there at the time. After they got Drake up off the floor
and left. I went to the doctor's office then to my mom's house. I was
on crutches for almost a week, and I could hardly walk. I tried to keep
it from my brother but how could I when I was staying with mom for
a while? They were in and out visiting mom. When Drake found out
that I was at my mom's house, he showed up asking my two sisters that
went to the door if he could talk to me. Wilma and Bell wanted to jump
on him so badly, but I talked them out of it. They asked me if I wanted
to talk to him and I said it was okay. Wilma and Bell told Drake that
he better not hit me. I went out to talk to him and he didn't like the
answers I was giving him for the questions he was asking so he shoved
me and both crutches went out from under me. I hit the storage room
door that I was standing in front of. My sisters ran out of the house.
He threw his hands up and said to them, "I didn't touch her, she fell."
A lie was something that came easy for Drake. My sisters asked him
to leave, and he did. I begged my sisters not to tell anyone what had
just happened, and they said they will try. The next thing I knew my
brother, Jerry, came up to the house. He was upset because he couldn't
find Drake anywhere after saying he had been looking for him all over
town. Jerry said that this town is not that big, and he could not find
that fellow nowhere. I was so glad to hear that he couldn't find him. I
made a call to his mom, and she told me he had gone back to work in St.
Louis. I was so relieved to hear her say that. That will give my brother
a chance to cool off. I didn't have anything else to do with Drake from
that point on. I felt that any man than would hit a lady was not worth

41

the time of day. I have always said that if God had wanted man to beat on a woman, he would have let him be born with a club in his hand. Ladies, we are better than that, we should be treated like queens. The same goes for the men that is if they are real men, they should be treated like a king. One day I will find my king. Drake and I would not have made it anyway, his drinking was really bad. My brother, Jerry, was still waiting to see him; he would ask me every once in a while, if I heard from him. Of course, I wouldn't have told him if I had but I earnestly did not hear from him. I went back home after I got off the crutches, but mom did not want me to go. She was worried about me so I told her that I will pack up and come home later. The rent was paid up so I could take my time.

About a week later I broke out in a really bad rash from some medication I was taking. Mom swore up and down that someone had hoodooed me. She was so upset. I tried to make her understand that it was the medicine. I broke out into blisters and the blisters dried into a black scalp on my face, chest and back. I looked a hot mess! When my sister Wilma and her husband came by, her husband jumped back and said, "oh you scared me." I ended up going to a Dermatologist for my skin. It wasn't my doctor's fault as far as I knew because I told him I was not allergic to anything. I can not say that now that I know. It is written down on my chart and any paperwork relating to my health and I don't ever want to go through that again. I still have a few spots left from the rash, nothing compared to what it was. My friend, Pablo, was so thoughtful and nice at that time. He made sure I got everything I needed while I was stuck inside the house. I didn't want to go out until my skin cleared up some.

CHAPTER

8

LOSING MY BROTHER JERRY

I lost my brother, Jerry, that year. That day for some reason I had the jitters or something. I just could not sit still. I did not feel like myself all day that day. Late that evening, I heard a knock on the door, and it was my brother Russel and his girlfriend Emily. Russel asked me if anyone had called or been by and I said, no. He got quiet for a minute and that was not like him. He was always talking. I asked Russel what was wrong. He looked at me with tears in his eyes and said, "Jerry is gone!" He had to catch me to keep me from falling. I asked him where my brother is now, and he told me that they had taken his body to the funeral home. I then ask where mom was right now, Russel said mom was still at the hospital when he left. It hurt me so bad. My brother was gone, and I did not have a chance to see him alive for the last time.

I had to focus on my mom and the rest of the family because everyone was so angry. I always felt in my heart that all the fighting they did would end up in a bad way; but never thought about it being deadly. I was not there, and I don't know what happened, but I was told that Jerry was getting in the truck with some of his co-workers which was a bunch of men. He was going to the company party that he worked for. I was told by my family that he was shot in a main artery and bled to death. What actually happened out there at that house we will never really know the truth, but God knows. We had to keep a close eye on my mom because she was not doing well at all. That was not a good day for my mom at all. She has lost her son through tragedy, now she's asking the woman who killed him why. I could not imagine in a million years how my mom was hurting. I am trying to console mom as we were walking away. I wanted to cry but I couldn't, I don't know if I was too angry or still in shock.

The day of the funeral was the worst day of my life. I kept telling myself that I was going to wake up. The church was so packed that day. I remember having to sit up front in the pews where the deacons of the church sat at that time. I was in a daze, but I remember my sister Stella and my brother-in-law, Parker, coming over to get me when it was time to view my brother's body for the last time. I remember getting up walking over to the casket. I don't remember anything else. When I woke up, I was in the back seat of my cousin's car and my sister was fanning me. I held my anger in too long. I knew exactly what it was. When we got to the burial grounds I did not want to get out; I knew I needed to think of my mom. I would not have been able to control myself, so I stayed in the car. Drake's mom and sister came over to sit for a while. Drake did not make it to the funeral, and I was glad of that.

When I did get a chance to sit down and talk to mom, she expressed to me that it is really hard seeing your child leave here before she did. She also told me that she knew something was going on with Jerry the time when he took his gold off his tooth. She talked also about one Easter Sunday when he came by the house with Hazel. We were all telling him how good he looked in the suit he was wearing. He said to mom, "This is the suit I want to be buried in." Mom said, "Don't say that baby," I told mom I remembered it like it was yesterday because the day he took the gold off his tooth he called me outside and asked me if I saw anything different about him. I did not until he told me, I could not believe it because he loved his gold tooth. But I never thought anymore about it. I especially remember that Easter Sunday how sharp he was and him saying that to mom. Mom said that was a sign when he did not want his gold anymore. I asked mom why is that? She then tells me that it has been said that when death is on a person, things that they have always cherished or loved will not mean anything to you anymore. I told her I never knew that. Mom never got over that; that is when her health started failing. The death of my brother, Jerry, was hard for everyone.

My brother left behind two daughters and a son. Mom said she was going to let God handle her. I want to mention that the suit that my brother Jerry said he wanted to be buried in, they had to cut it off of him the day he died. Y'all, I have got to leave this alone. It seemed like it was only yesterday. That is why when things seem to go wrong, I always recite the Prayer of Serenity; God grant me the serenity to accept the things I cannot change, the courage to change the things I can, and the wisdom to know the difference. I have missed my brother so much over the years. It was years before I laid eyes on my nieces and nephew. God blessed me with the strength and courage to go back out to the house. I cannot explain to you how I felt. God is good; He will equip you with what you need. "Thank you, God!"

My sister, Clara, had a baby that year. She got married and moved in her own place. It was a baby girl. Mom told her if she had known she was pregnant she would not have let her go to our brother Jerry's funeral. Clara said to mom that she would still have wanted to go. Everyone was going through so many different emotions. I thank God that no one else got hurt during this time in our lives. Imagine trying to keep an eye out for everybody, especially my other brothers. The only time they settled down was when mom called them together and told them to let the Lord handle it. She also told them that she would not be able to take it if something else would happen. After that, everyone quieted down.

I had packed up and moved back home with mom when Drake showed up at the door one day. He asked me what was going on because he went by the house, and no one was there. I told him that I did not see a reason to stay at the house and try to pay all the bills by myself. He did not know that I had also gotten a divorce while he was off in

St. Louis enjoying his life. There was an attorney that was an expert in divorce cases; her name was Ms. Stapleton. The day I went to her and told her my situation, she told me that she was going to put an ad in the paper and if he does not answer within thirty days, I will automatically get my divorce. Believe me, after thirty days she called me to pick up my divorce papers. I told Drake to wait a few minutes. I came back to the door with the divorce papers, and he asked me what is that? These are our divorce papers. Ms. Stapleton, the lawyer, the one that does divorces, will give you a copy of it. He looks at me and tells me that I will always be his wife and no paperwork will ever change that. I told him. "how did you expect me to stay with you and you abandoned me." He said, "I did not abandon you; I was foolish and was not thinking. I was listening to what everybody was telling me. I just did not know what else to do so I stopped sending money home." So, I asked him why he did not talk to me. I was the best person to ask. I told him that there was no way that I could trust him again. A relationship without trust is not a relationship. He drops his head and walked away. As he was walking away, he said again to me, "you will always be my wife."

I started working at Kurt's Restaurant on Highway 12. I was a short order cook. It took me a while to get everything together; but I finally did. Instead of them calling it a short order cook, it should have been called a fast order cook. Once I got the hang of it, I was good. Pablo and I continued to see each other after the divorce. It wasn't anything serious, not to me anyway. I was focusing on myself at that time. Pablo did not stay in town; he lived about twenty-nine miles east of Price. He lived in Wayland, Mississippi and I never wanted to get serious about anybody that lived out of town.

CHAPTER

9

MEETING MALCOLM AND ALL THE CHAOS I WENT THROUGH

There was this guy whose name was Malcolm Smith, and he would approach me from time to time with a small conversation, never anything of importance. On this particular Sunday as I was getting out of my car when he pulls up. He asked me how was I doing, and my response was 'Ok', how are you? He said he would do better if I would go out with him for dinner. By me being the person I am, even though Pablo and I were not really dating, I told him maybe another time. I have always been a one-man woman and I needed to straighten some things out with Pablo before I would even consider going out with him. Pablo was not coming around much at that time. I think that he saw more into our relationship than I did. When he did come to town, we had a long talk about our relationship and what was what. Pablo said he knew our relationship was not going to work because he did not live near. He wanted us to continue to be friends and just friends. So, we both agreed on it.

The next time I saw Malcolm, I told him that I would go out with him. There was one date after another, we became close in a short period to time. He was always a gentleman. I had some people to tell me he was not the kind of guy I needed. Of course, I followed my own mind, I believe in giving people the benefit of the doubt. As time went on things began to show up; everywhere we went everybody knew him. I asked him one day did he know everybody in town? Malcolm looked at me and said, "just about, is there a problem with that!" I looked at him and said no I don't have a problem with that. I also told him that he did not have to be so serious. That was when we started having problems; or should I say, that is when I started really paying attention to things.

I started classes at Priestly Hospital on a 4-12 shift. I could not get in the house some nights without Malcolm pulling up in the driveway, saying he was checking to make sure I got in the house safely. I admit it was nice to see him. On weekends, we all would sit out under the tree in the front yard. Everybody would be blowing their horns and speaking. Everybody knew my family because we are a big family. My sister Wilma's husband, Gary, looked over at me and started laughing asking me did I see my competition pass by. I asked him who he was talking about. He said that the lady that just passed by was my competition. I did not see who he was talking about, so, I did not question it anymore; I said time will tell it all.

Malcolm would take me out a lot to different clubs and on picnics. We were always going somewhere; we had fun together. Things started to hit the fan, as my dad use to say, we began having so many ups and downs. Sometimes, I would talk to Pablo about the things I was going through but never everything though. The first thing he will say is I am here for you if you need me, and I appreciated that. I just did not want him to get the wrong signal. I came to realize that Malcolm was a ladies' man. He had a good heart, but when it came to lying, he was the master. I remember one night we went out dancing and we could not dance for different women pushing and hitting him in the back. I would lose my step so much when I danced with him it got so that I did not want to dance with him at all. Sometimes, I wanted to go to the movies or to the bowling alley, but I could count on one hand the number of times we went to the movies. I started getting phone calls. They would ask for me and would not say a word; just holding the phone. It was as if whoever it was, was looking at me. The calls came before and after work. I mentioned it to Malcolm, and he said he had not idea who that could be. However, that was the answer I expected from him.

My sister Wilma's friend, Rylee, told me one day that she did not know what it was about me, but Malcolm seemed to care more about me than any woman she has known him to date. I looked at her and said to myself, if only she knew. My sister and Rylee worked together. They also car-pooled together along with some other co-workers. One morning on their way to work, Wilma called me to tell me she saw his car parked at someone's house. She said to me that it looked like it had been there all night. It was cold and you can tell if a car had been sitting all night or not. She told me where his car was, and I got up to go see for myself. It was his car, and she was right. I knew Malcolm would lie, so I did not ask him about it. I found out who it was later as time went on. Her name is Willow. I had heard rumors about her, but I saw it for myself; he was just unbelievable. I was supposed to go out with him that Friday night, but something came up. I finished what I had to do, and my sister Millie and I rode out to the club where he was. As we turned into the parking lot, we saw him sitting on the hood of his car and a girl was between his legs with her arms wrapped around his neck. I read his lips when he told her that I was pulling up, and she tore off running. That was when I put two and two together. So, that was where the phone calls were coming from. Remember me telling you that whoever it was calling me, it was as if they knew when I was home. She was always walking pass the house going to the store. So, after she takes off running, I get out of the car and asked him what he was doing. He would not answer me. Whatever he was drinking in his cup, when he turned it up again, I hit the bottom of the cup and it went down his chest, up his nose and all over him. I took off running and he was chasing me around the cars in the parking lot. I got back to my car and told Millie to go, lets get out of here! Millie locked the doors and we left. He was pointing and yelling at me saying that this wasn't over.

It is now the week of graduation from the classes I was taking at Priestly Hospital. Mom sent me to the store to pick up some things for her. On my way back, there his car was parked in a lady's yard. who lived around the corner from me. By this time, I am just really fed up with him. So, I stopped, and he comes running over to my car. I asked him what was going on and why was he at Zoe's house knowing all along he was going to lie. This man tells me that Zoe and he was getting ready to go get me a graduation gift. I told him you must think I am dumb or something. I told him that lie did not even sound right to him. I asked him to get away from the car and go on with where he was going. Zoe was a nice girl and she and I never had any problems. I thought of Zoe as a friend. Malcolm came the next day with candy and a teddy bear; he always came up with something thinking I would forgive him. That is the kind of person he was, but it was getting old. He at one time thought I was seeing someone because I started finding other things to do. There wasn't another man, but to be sure I could not turn for him being there. He would hang around until he thought he had run someone off. Then he would go back to his old games. Let me tell you, I don't know why I put up with that man the way I did. For one, I just loved his mom; she was the sweetest person you could ever meet. As time went on the girl that my sister Wilma's husband had mentioned the day in the front yard about her being my competition surfaced. Her name was Everly. She was going around telling people that Malcolm was going to buy her an engagement ring for Christmas. When I ask Malcolm what was going on between the two of them, you and I know what the answer was. He said I don't know that woman is crazy. I told him that she wasn't saying that for no reason; we will find out Christmas since it was only a few months away; you know how people do talk. Malcolm wasn't talking much these days and I did not ask him why. I was over to his house one day and this girl Everly shows up. She knocks and knocks but he would not open the door. I asked him why he wouldn't answer the door if there was nothing going on between them there would be nothing to hide. He didn't open the door and she soon left. He did not know but that told me a lot; he was hiding something.

My sister Clara's husband, Milton, and Malcolm were good friends, and we would play cards at their house almost every weekend. This particular weekend on a Saturday afternoon, everyone was sitting around the table playing cards and someone knocked on the door. My brother-in-law, Milton, answered the door and tells Malcolm that someone wanted to see him. This was a girl I had not heard of or seen before. My brother-in-law said to me not to pay any attention to her, but I am hearing this girl saying to Malcolm that he was supposed to have come by the house to give her money for the kids some shoes. Tell me how would I ignore this? I do not know what he said to her, but she left. I never believed that children should be in the midst of foolishness. So, I asked Malcolm who she was, do you believe he told me that he had children by her, and her name was Lucy. He said she lived over near my aunt Caroline. Aunt Caroline lived on Scarlett St. I am looking at him and saying so my aunt knows that you are a whorish man, it looks like everybody in town knew but me. I was so upset with him that day, I felt like I could spit bullets. I got up getting ready to leave and my sister Clara is trying to calm me down. I told her I would be okay, and I suggested to Malcolm that he needed to get up and go take care of his responsibilities. He kept trying to talk to me, but this time I was not listening. I did not talk to him I know for about three days. We usually would talk every day. I was so tired of this merry-go-round I was on, how much more am I going to put up with. I said to myself that I must really love this man, or something is wrong with me. One thing I can say about him is that he had a good heart and was a gentleman in every way. When I did talk to Malcolm, he just explained himself away. He said he would have told me about his children's momma if he thought it was important, that his past should not have anything to do with me. I asked him how he could think I did not want to know that he had children; that is very important to me. How can you say something like that, what are you trying to hide now?

It is the day before Christmas and believe it or not Malcolm and I went out. We had a good time. When we got back to the house, he pulls out a gift from his pocket and gives it to me. It was an engagement ring; this is the ring that the girl Everly was telling everybody she was going to get. There was complete silence for a minute. Then I told him that it was a beautiful ring. I played it off saying 'thank you' to him. He kept asking me if I knew what the ring represented. I would just say 'yes, I know'. It was not a week later when I heard about him at the club with another woman, a married woman, I might add. Word was, he had been dating this woman for years. I was told that everybody in town knew about them, and I am like yeah, everybody but me. The lady's name I was told was Mrs. Donna Soto. I remember seeing the lady around town but did not know her name. I can remember how I would sometimes catch her staring at me, but never thought anything of it. Out of all the things he did or was into, he did not want anyone around me.

One evening Pablo called and said he was in town and wanted to stop by to see me. I had gotten ready for bed, so I told him I will put on my robe and come out. Who pulls up in the driveway behind us, but Malcolm? At first, he just sit there, and Pablo asked me who he was. I told him it was Malcolm. He gets out of his car and walks up to the care, first on Pablo's side and said, 'good evening.' Then, he comes to my side of the car and just started going off, asking question after question. He wanted to know why I was sitting in the car this time of night with my bed clothes on. Out of all the things I had gone through with this man, he was questioning me. Pablo and I was only talking, and I don't think it was fifteen minutes later before Malcolm pulls up. I tried to explain that to him, but why am I trying to explain anything? Malcolm goes back to his car and just sits there. Pablo asked me did I think that he would let him out, I said I did not see why not. Pablo cranks up his car letting him know that he wanted to get out. By then, I have gotten out of the car getting ready to go back in the house. Malcolm just sits there; not moving. So, I walks to his car and asked him to let Pablo out. He hesitated for a minute but did move. How could he act like this, I was thinking to myself? I knew then that I was going to have to break things off with him. He was unbelievable as I said once before. Pablo called me the next morning to tell me he followed him to the county line on his bumper. Wow! That was it. I am through. I eventually got away from him. I heard he was dating someone that he had been seeing also, like I said everybody else knew but me. He was dating so many women. The day I walked away from Malcolm, I told him that there is going to come a day when he is going to wish he could just look me in my face, and I am not going to be anywhere around. He looked at me and said to let him worry about that. I had to walk away; I needed some kind of peace in my life.

About a year later, I heard rumors that Malcolm was engaged to be married. I was happy for him, so I called to congratulate him on his engagement. You will not believe what he told me when I congratulated him. This man tells me that is what he heard! I told him that I was going to hang up the phone because he was lying. I told him that if it was a lie, it looks like to me that he was the one to straighten it out. I laughed at him and hung up the phone. Malcolm had gotten so quiet, my brother-in-law or no one had heard anything from him. The day this man is supposed to get married, he calls me and tells me the same thing again. I told him to call her by her name, Josephine. I then asked him what time is your wedding, shouldn't you be at the church? He sounded so serious that day on the phone. He told me that he loved me, and he had so many emotions going on within him. I said that I did not know what he wanted me to say to him. I told him that I can not make him any promises, that I am going to put myself in your soon-to-be wife, Josephine's place. You need to get up and go to that church. This is not the day to be getting all these mixed emotions, I wished him the best and I hung up the phone.

CHAPTER

MEETING EARL WHILE WORKING AT PRIESTLY HOSPITAL

My work kept me pretty busy. Priestly Hospital was a place where you could advance if you stayed there long enough. I met a guy that seemed to be nice. We started talking and getting to know each other, but he failed to tell me that he had a baby by one of the girls that worked on the floor. His name was Earl. Earl was a quiet laid-back kind of guy. The day that this girl he had a baby by saw us together, she yelled out, "did y'all see that!" That was when he told me he had a baby by her, but I asked him why he didn't tell me that when we first started talking. He goes on to tell me that there was nothing between them and it had not been for years. So, I did not ask him anything else about her. She did not work on the same floor, so that was a good thing. I thought of Earl as more of a friend, but realized he thought different. He lived about an hour away, but you would have thought he lived around the corner. He was always here in Price with me. Later on, he started talking about moving in with me; everything was moving a little too fast for me. When I told him about how I was feeling, he was not too happy about it at all. But we both agreed to give it some more time. We did grow closer as time passed, but still not enough to move in together. I figured that was a big step to be taking with him. Later on, we had the same conversation and now it was getting repetitious, so, I said to him that maybe we should give each other a break for a while. That was when he turned into somebody else. He would show up wherever I was out of the blue; it was as if he was watching me. We soon began to drift apart. I knew that it would not last. Earl got so ridiculous that he showed up one Sunday morning at my church and joined the church. I was so outdone. I could not speak. My mom looked at me and asked me if that was him and I said yes. While they were giving him right-hand fellowship, I went to get mom's glasses she had left a home. By the time I made it to the stop sign around the corner from the house, he was on my bumper. He wanted me to stop but I would not. He just made me nervous, I just couldn't trust him. He has been so aggressive the last few times we talked. I drove up to my sister, Millie's, house and got out of the car and went inside the house. He got out of his car, came in behind me and ran me all around my sister's house. She asked him to leave because she did not want any trouble. He did leave out of the house and went back to sit in his car. Millie asked me what was going on and I told her he just changed on me. I just came to pick up mom's glasses and take them back to church. When Earl finally left, I ran to the car to go get mom's glasses. When I returned, mom asked me what took me so long to go and come back, I just could not tell her the truth. She thought Earl was a nice guy. He was always bringing her something and he made her the biggest chest to go at the foot of her bed. That was the only side she saw; I saw the other side.

One day while giving one of the patients a bath, I broke my wrist. I did not know it was that bad until my hand started to swell. I remember having to pull my hand from under her arm because she was clinching it and would not let go. I ended up going on to the emergency room after my supervisor kept telling me I needed to go. After the doctor took the X-rays, he told me that my wrist was crumbled like chalk. I could not believe what he was telling me. I got scheduled for surgery about a week later. It was so boring recuperating at home. I was so glad when it was time to go back to work. I went back on light duty until I was released from the doctor. I went to therapy for weeks; I loved the hot wax treatments. I managed to officially get away from Earl. It was not easy at all; he tried every trick in the book. Being back at work felt so good. I got promoted to Alternate Supervisor after getting the required hours at the local college. It was a change for me, but I soon learned my job. I had eighteen ladies that I supervised; some that did not care much for me because they were older ladies. It did not matter how I made the schedule there was always something wrong with it. I caught it with them until they realized I was not going anywhere. We all eventually started getting along; we became a big happy family.

I was in therapy one day and as I was walking in the room, a guy walked out. He looked at me and took off. When he came back in, he just sit down and stared at me. I acted as if I did not see him staring, but it was so annoying. He finally came over and asked me what my name was and that he didn't mean to stare but I looked like somebody he knew. He was there for his elbow; he had fallen off a ladder. We talked for a minute and exchanged phone numbers before he left. There was a big difference in our ages. We started talking over the phone and enjoyed talking to each other. From that point on, we were inseparable. I just knew my mom was not going to like him. Mom was only a few years older than he was and I was not believing this myself. The first time I told her about him, she looked at me and said that you can't tell your heart who to love. I never thought you would date anybody that age. His name was Pace Steele and he lived in a little town called Dreary, Mississippi. Dreary, Mississippi was about an hour or so east of Price. The first time he came to visit, he got here so fast that mom said to him," I thought you said he lived an hour away." She said you were just on the phone with him, and we both laughed about it. Mom seemed to like him, but sometimes it is hard to tell, so I asked her, and she said that he seemed to be alright. I did not like Dreary County at all. It think it had one store and one gas station. It was a big change from Price. Pace was an only child. His mom was Ms. Sarah Benson. She was a nice lady and we got along good. About four months into our relationship, Pace asked me to marry him which I thought at first, he was just talking, but he was serious. We loved each other enough but moving to Dreary County was not what I wanted to do. When I talked to my mom about it, she said that it is a wife's place to be with her husband. I knew she was going to say something like that. She was happy for us and that we might make a good couple. Pace had his own house and land that was paid for, but I just did not like that little town, y'all!

The day we told his mom that we were getting married, she looked at me and asked me if I was sure I wanted to marry her son. I said to her, "yes, I am sure." She shrugged her shoulders and said, "ok." I didn't mentioned it to Pace because I did not want him to ask her about it. But believe me, it stayed on my mind. I said to myself that one day I would ask her about it. Another thing she kept saying was that she could not believe we were getting married. Pace heard her say that, but never gave a response. His grandmother was a pure jewel. Her name was Precious Steele. Her name fit her very well. She and Pace's uncle lived up the road from him. His uncle's name Jasper Steele: he was nice too. There were several other uncles that lived in the North. Pace's dad was the only son who was deceased. She did not have any girls. That was probably why Pace's grandma liked me so much. She gave me her wedding veil to wear on my wedding day which really touched me. We got married in the backyard at my mom's house. It was a nice wedding, but none of his family showed up. I thought that was really strange and so did my family. They never asked about it afterwards. When I asked Pace about it, his only response was, "I don't know." Going to Dreary County that day was not something I looked forward to. I could hear my mom's voice in the back of my mind telling me it was my place to go with him.

The house sat way back off the road. We passed by his grandma's and uncle's house to get to our house. They lived up the hill from us. I could not understand the relationship between Pace and his mom; you would think by him being the only child that there would be a special bond. Pace and I were members at his family church, St. Mathis Church. Pace had two other uncles that lived in Dreary County, Uncle Bill Steele and Uncle Roger Steele. Uncle Bill's wife's name was Hannah and they both were very sweet ladies. Uncle Roger was the preacher in the family. He had the heaviest voice I had ever heard at that time. Everyone always went to him for guidance and prayer. He was an awesome man, I thought.

One Sunday morning while getting dressed for church, I was having a hard time buttoning my skirt, so I asked Pace to try and button it. He said he could not button it either and that I had been eating too much. I never thought much about it again until the next Sunday one dress that was always a little big on me was too tight. That was when I started thinking and my first thought was, I am pregnant. I was not going to say anything to Pace until, I was sure. I made an appointment at the Health Department and a week later I found out that I was an expectant mother. Pace was so excited when I told him. He said, "I am having a baby at my age, wow!" Pace's mom was excited as well as his grandma and uncles. They kept talking about a new baby on the Steele place is really awesome. I had some good months, a little nausea but not much. For eight months I had no pain, no swelling or anything. The only things I did was gain weight; with my first pregnancy, I really did not know what to expect. I think I called my mom every day. She understood what I was going through being a mother of fourteen. When that last month hit, I caught it. I hurt every day, all day. I went to the hospital twice in false labor. My doctor gave me some medicine to stop my labor the second time I went to the hospital. He said it was too early for me to go in labor that my baby's lungs had not developed enough. That was on the twelfth day of June. She was not due until the twenty-second of July. I had the flu when I had my daughter, so they had to do a C-Section because I had not been eating and her heart rate was shallow. I had a temperature of 102 and they would not let me hold her or bring her near me. God took care of my little girl and me. We named our daughter Delilah. Delilah was born at one-thirty in the morning. When I opened my eyes my mom and brother, Walter, was there. I cannot tell you how happy I was to see them. It's something about seeing your mom at times like that.

At six o'clock, I was up walking to the nursery to see my daughter but had no idea where I was going. I looked up and two or three nurses were running toward me with a wheelchair. I just froze, all I could hear was, "Mrs. Steele, Mrs. Steele don't move." One nurse said, "Lord, look at this woman!" She asked me was I trying to get them fired. What are you doing out of the bed already, you have got to be some kind of woman, you just had a C-Section earlier? She said, "please sit down, I will take you to the nursery." When we made it to the nursery, the nurse asked me if I knew which baby was mine. I told her the one with her head up looking around. The nurse asked me how I knew. I said I just knew. My doctor came in the room looking for me to be in the bed, but I was in the chair watching television. My doctor's name was Dr. Miller. Dr. Miller had so many patients. He was very attractive and may I add, single. He said to me that it look like you are doing good if you are up, you can go home tomorrow. I didn't know how my daughter would know me because Pace stayed in the nursery all the time. He stopped by the nursery before he came to the room, which was okay. The nurse came to the room to tell me that my baby was not eating like she should; so, I asked her to bring her in the room with me. I kept her in the room with me until I left the hospital.

We stopped by Pace mom's house on our way from the hospital, she said she wanted to see her grandbaby. She was so happy to see us. Pace told her not to touch her because she had not washed her hands. I asked him not to do her like that, she was just excited. I did understand about the putting your hands on a baby's hand the only thing they know is to put their hand in their mouth. I asked him to just wipe Delilah's hand with a wet wipe it will be okay. I needed to go out to get some things for the baby, so Pace's cousin, Ava, who was his uncle Bill's daughter, came to stay until I got back. My mom would have gotten on me if she knew I was out that early. I really appreciated Ava coming over that day. There is no way Pace would have known what to get. Later on in the week, Pace's Uncle Bill and Aunt Liza came to see Delilah. As time went on, Pace's mother would always say that Delilah was getting dark. When she kept mentioning it, I asked him why she always said that. Pace told me that his mom was stuck on color, and she was color-struck. I laughed at him thinking he was joking. He said that when he was a boy his mom used Jergen's lotion on him thinking it would keep him from changing colors. I never really thought about color. As long as my daughter was healthy, color did not matter to me. Delilah have color like the Steele side of the family.

Delilah started having problems with her breathing when she was about a year and a half. I took her to the children's hospital for allergy testing. There were so many things she was allergic too. She had a very bad case of asthma, even to the point where she would stop breathing. I had to call 911 one day. There was no ambulance service in Dreary County; they did not know how I reached them. All I know is they showed up in the front yard. The ambulance driver said he did not understand it either, it just came over their radio. I know that it was God; nobody but Him. I have thanked Him a many days for being there for us. Delilah got better over the years with her asthma. The doctor told me to remember that asthma never goes away, it just gets better. I had been thinking about going back to work for a while and finally talked it over with Pace. He insisted that I needed to be home with Delilah. I would mention it every now and then and Pace would always change the subject. I was so used to working that I wanted to do something. Pace got a little tired of me bring it up so he said to me if I got someone reliable to babysit Delilah that we would give it a try. While talking to Pace and Aunt Liza one day, she told me that Pace's cousin, Cora, was a babysitter. So, I called her to see if she would be willing to be Delilah's babysitter once I found a job. She agreed to, so I started putting in applications. I started working at a nursing home in Dreary County. I worked for Riggly Nursing Home. Everything was working out until one day I picked Delilah up and there was a long scratch on her face. Pace was not happy at all; he wanted me to quit my job. He said if I was going to work, we would have to work around Delilah. Pace worked six until two on his job, so I started the three to eleven shift. Things was running smoothly for about a year. Pace decided he wanted me home at night, so he worked a four to twelve shifts, and I went to days. I was not happy with being at home at night with us being so far off the highway. This job also would take him out of town sometimes. He did this for about two years before he got another promotion and did not have to go out of town anymore. Pace's mom's brother passed away who lived in Chicago, Illinois. His name was Uncle Sanchez whom I never met. Pace's mom was the only girl. All of Pace's uncles came home to see his mom. That was when I found out how strange his mom really was and their relationship. He talked about it saying that was how she was. I said to him how could she be like that; you were her only child. I just did not understand at all. She bought her a trailer and Pace had it put on our land. He said she was getting too old to stay by herself and we will be right across the yard from each other if she need help.

About a month later, Pace asked me did I think we needed a vacation which I agreed to. I am thinking that his job had given him a big raise. Our first stop was Look Out Mountain in Tennessee. We stayed there overnight at the Hilton Hotel. The next morning, we got up heading to St. Louis to Grant's Farm. We had a ball, especially, the girls. We took one of the neighbor's daughters with us. She and Delilah had become good friends. We saw the Clydesdale horses take out; everybody called them the Budweiser horses. It was so much to see. I mean we were from one state to another. Pace kept stopping at

different ATM machines, the first thing I said to myself was his job is good to have given him this raise. I did not ask, and he did not tell. We left St. Louis and went on to Chicago, Illinois, New York and then to Pittsburgh, Pennsylvania. We stayed at the best hotels and ate the best of goods. I decided that I was going to ask him where he was getting so much money from. That was when he decided to tell me that his mom got her ATM card in the mail and did not know what it was. I was so shocked at what he was telling me. I told him that God is not going to bless us for that and I am in the midst of it. I was really hurting behind this. If I had only known, I would have tried to talk him out of it. I could not enjoy the rest of that vacation. I just wish I had never asked Pace that question. I kept thinking if he did his mom like that, what would he do to me. "Oh my God!"

A week later, Pace's mom called me crying in the phone asking me where her son was. Before I could say anything, she started to tell me how Pace had taken money out of the bank. She asked me did I know about it. I had to know if he was spending a lot of money. I was just lost for words. I told her that when I found out that the damaged had already been done and that I was really sorry. She talked to Pace and hung up the phone. I don't know what was said, I went to the other room. She called me back and asked me if I could take her to the bank. She was going to get her money and they knew not to give her money to her son. She was not in a good state of mind. I thought she was going to have Pace locked up. I did not know what to think at that time.

On this particular day, we were just sitting talking when she asked me did my son tell you what happened between, he and his cousin? I told her that he never mentioned anything to me. She told me that she would tell me, but she was scared that I would tell him. She did tell me that Pace's cousin don't want to have anything to do with him. I said to her that whatever happened it must have been bad.

One day I got a phone call from my sister Millie. She told me that Malcolm had been worrying her to death so much so that she had to call me to get him off her back. She also said that he had been worrying the whole family. Millie asked me not to be mad with her but just talk to him for a minute and he was standing there beside her. I told her he knows that I am married and so is he; what could he possible want. She gave him the phone and the only thing he kept saying to me was he just wanted to see me. Before it was over, I did agree to meet him so that my family could have some peace. When we met up, I told him this right off that I was faithful to my husband. He hugged me and I did not think he was going to ever let me go. I asked him did he remember me telling him that there will come a day that you are going to want to look me in my face and I am not going to be nowhere around? He said, yes, I remember you saying that to me.

I told him that the day has come, and I am going to tell you the same thing that I told you on your wedding day, "I can't make you any promises." He began to tell me how things were with him and his wife. I did not want to hear about that. I told him to go back home to his wife and try to make things work. I wished him the best and moved on.

Pace's mom had a nurse to come out to check her sugar and take her blood pressure. She sometimes would not let the nurse in the house. The nurse would just stand there knocking and she said that she could see her standing there looking at her. Her name was Abigail. Abigail and I would talk from time to time. She told me one day that I don't know but I married into a crazy family. She said that all these people go crazy before they die but don't worry you will see. I laughed at her at first until I realized that she was serious. I am saying to myself, do she really know what she is talking about. For some reason, this stayed with me. Abigail and her family lived in the bend of the road where we came into the house. Her dad owned horses and sometimes would come down the road riding them, they were beautiful.

It was time for Delilah to start Head start. I did not know who was more excited, me or Delilah. She already knew her numbers and alphabets. She could read small sentences as well. I had been working with her very faithfully. Delilah got a Citizenship Award her first year in school. She learned to read really well over the summer. She was in the library competitions where she won second place in the most books read that summer. Delilah always made honor roll when she started first grade. I was so very proud of her.

Pace's mom passed away a year later. The doctor said it was her lung. Pace nor I was there when she passed. The nurse gave me her ring and watch saying to me that she said she wanted her daughter-in-law to have it. That really touched my heart. She was such a sweet person. I do wish she had told me what happened between Pace and his cousin. I know that he will never tell. Delilah was too young to know what was going on even though I did tell her that her grandma was in heaven with Jesus. I let Pace handle the arrangements and everything. I was there for him if he needed me. We did not want the trailer to just sit there, so we stayed sometimes in the trailer and sometimes in the house. The first year after Pace's mom passed, he seemed to start changing on me. We went everywhere together, but all of a sudden, he was going by himself. He started doing things that he had never done. I thought one time that he had started secretly drinking but he had not. I never saw any signs of another woman, not saying that it wasn't happening. When I knew something was going on was at my yearly exam. The doctor told me she did not want me to go home and jump on my husband, but he was having intercourse with more than me. On my way out of the doctor's office, I felt so dirty. I got home and confronted him with it. His answer was that the doctor didn't know what she is talking about. I got even angrier at him because he was talking to me like I was stupid. I mean he cried and trust to swear on his mama's grave. That did it, I was on my way back home to Price. I let him think that I was ok, oh I was so nice. I put up this pretense for about a month at the same time I was slowly packing Delilah and my clothes. I had already talked to mom about what was going on. She was worried about me, but I promised her that I was going to be alright. I knew that I will be gone sooner than she thought.

Pace left that Saturday morning saying that he was going to Louisiana. By he time I thought he might be on the highway, Delilah and I left going back to Price. I had packed enough clothes for the both of us. I felt a sense of relief when I drove away from that house. My daughter was young and did not understand. I did want to see her grow up with her daddy, but circumstances changed. It takes two to make a marriage. I did not know how tired I was until I left Dreary County. When Pace got home, he called and asked me where I was. I told him that we were in Price. Oh, he just blew up, telling me that I did not tell him that I was leaving. I had to end up hanging up on him because he was getting out of hand. He kept calling and asking when I was coming back home. I told him that we were not coming back. He then asked me if I was crazy; that I had taken his daughter away from him. It just blew me away. All of a sudden, we were important again. I knew I was not going back because I had started looking for a job. The first application I put in was who called me. It was a local nursing home in Price. Price County Nursing Home wasn't a bad place to work. I worked the seven to three shift at first. I got a call from Price School District and that was when I went to three to eleven at Price County Nursing Home. So, I worked full time on both jobs for a while. When Malcolm found out I was back in town, I could not rest for him. He worked on the same grounds at Price Hospital which was right across in front of me. I continued to stand my ground with Malcolm. I just did not want anything to do with another woman's husband. I was still married to Pace also. Every lunch break when I got off there was Malcolm. I had to leave Price County Nursing Home. I needed some peace. It was too much going on in my life. The more I told him that, the worse he got. He did not act like he wanted to understand. That was just how he was.

After working for a few months, I decided that it was time for me to get my own place. Mom did not want me to go because she was still concerned about me. I thought I would first ask Pace if I could get the trailer that his mom wanted Delilah and I to have. That was a call I wished I had not made. He claimed that the trailer was not in good enough shape to move. I am knowing he is lying to me. There was not anything wrong with that trailer. I told him okay and hung up the phone. When I decided to go get my furniture, I had to take one of my brothers with me to the house. Practically everything in the house, I had when I married him, except for the washer and dryer. I was not shocked when I got there to see the trailer gone. He sold it to somebody in Magden, Mississippi. The same place where we got our van from. My brother, Walter, went with me to get my furniture. He asked me not to say anything, just get my stuff so we can go and that is what I did. I noticed that while my brother and I was getting the furniture, Pace and Walter did eventually had a long conversation. As I was getting ready to go, he asked me for my set of keys to the van. I wanted to really go off at that time. Walter asked me to let him have the keys, so I did. This was what the conversation they were so involved in must have been about. I left Dreary County not happy at all. I am just glad I did not have any problems getting my furniture. A few months later, one of the ladies I worked with at the nursing home in Dreary called me telling me how Pace was around telling everybody that I had taken all of his money and left. Her name was Henrietta. Henrietta was a down to earth person. She would tell me if no one else would. She said that she knew it wasn't true. He was only trying to make himself look good. I told her that he was lying and that he did not have any money for me to take. For the sake of my daughter, I tried to at least stay on speaking terms with him. He started lying to Delilah all the time. There were times when He was supposed to pick her up, but something always came up. He always had some lame excuse for not doing what he was supposed to do as her father. He would tell her when she would ask for something that your mother get money for you from me. I asked him what did that have to do with anything? I am raising a daughter you only have you. It cost to raise a child up. I wanted Delilah to have the things she needed. Pace was getting to the point where he was really working my nerves. I had to pray a lot. That reminded me of how mom would always say to me that when a man see that the woman don't want to have anything else to do with him, you will see how much he loves his children. She would tell me there are some real fathers that will be in their children's life no matter what. To the real fathers out there, I applaud you.

Delilah and I moved to an apartment complex that wasn't a mile from mom. Compton Heights were some nice apartments. I didn't like the parking situation over there, especially on the weekend. I lived in apartment G and had to park at apartment K, or L. I knew I wanted to move the first month I was there. I had a situation about a week after moving in. The neighbor from upstairs went to the office and expressed to the manager that I was taking up two parking spaces. When the manager knocked on the door, she was very nice about it. She asked me to move one of my vehicles in the parking space on the corner right across the street. She said I know you did not know because I did not tell you, but this lady is complaining. It was not a problem for me, I politely moved. So, now I know that I only have one parking spot. It would have been nice if the neighbor had come to me. Mrs. Audrey was a nice person; she was liked by all the tenants.

Malcolm was still up to his old tricks. Every chance he got, he tried to see me. It was just no giving up for him. I knew that the only way he was going to let up was for me to meet someone. I was not really ready for another relationship at the time. There was this guy who was a member of the church that showed interest in me, I just never showed him in anyway that I was interested. He seem to be a nice person. The next time he approached me, I did talk to him for a minute. We went out to eat one Saturday night. His name was Woodrow. We dated for about a year and a half and he asked me to marry him. I had not gotten a divorced from Pace yet. I knew it was time to get the divorce over with and I just did not want any drama to come up with Pace. I though that he was better since time had passed but was I wrong! When I told him that I had filed for a divorce, he told me that the only way I will sign is if you sign the van over to me. I do not know how he would think that would have been a problem for me. I did not want my Name on anything he had. We made arrangements to meet up in Dreary County when my lawyer was ready for him to sign the divorce papers. So, we were through with that, he signed my papers, and I signed his. I was determined to find out from him who he was seeing when we were together. I told him that he could tell me now that we were divorced. He told me that she was an older lady that was one of his clients. She always told him how nice he looked and how lucky I was to have a good-looking well-dressed man. That was what he said that got him to start seeing her. He asked me did I remember him going to one of his clients funeral and I said, yes. He said that his co-workers told him that he killed that old lady. When he laughed about it, I told him that it really wasn't funny, if its true. He said he did not know that she had a bad heart until after she died. I looked at him and said, 'Wow! Really!' After that conversation with him, I was just through.

Pace and Delilah's relationship did not get any better; he kept lying to her all the time. My mom always told us that one thing you don't do is talk against a child's daddy. So, I never talked against him to her, but I gave him the third degree all the time. He really started to get on my nerves. He one day asked me to meet him to get Delilah. I did not ask any questions, I met him. When he pulled up, he got this lady in the truck with him who was a supervisor at one of the restaurants in Dreary County. She was always ugly to me; could he have been courting her too. I did not ask any questions and he did not tell. I thought about the saying, 'you can't see the forest for the trees.'

CHAPTER

PACE MEETS WOODROW

Woodrow and I got married at my mom's house too. We were married in the living room. I did let Pace and Woodrow meet each other before we got married. Pace claimed he wanted to meet the man that was going to be in the house with his daughter. All of a sudden, he was concerned. My daughter wasn't too happy about me marrying him. You know how children are, they think mom is suppose to be with dad. Delilah stayed mad with me for years because she thought I left her dad. We stayed in the apartment for some months and then moved in our first home. The next day after we got married, Woodrow's ex-wife came by the apartment saying that he had left some things at her apartment on Sunday night, and she was there to return them. I told her to take them to him and whatever she had going on that I did not want any parts of it. I asked her to leave but before she left, she told me that he asked her to marry him again. I said to her that she should really be crazy because after asking you to marry him he still married me. That was when she decided to leave. There were situations all the time when it came to this lady. Back to the house we bought, we were excited about our first house. Woodrow started doing sneaky stuff early on after we moved in This house was on Sealy Street. Sealy Street was a short street, It probably had about seven or eight houses on it. I liked the house when I first saw it. One day Woodrow and I was outside, and his ex-girlfriend passed by the house. He came up with some excuse to leave. I laughed at him and said, I'm going to give him enough rope to hang himself. I had just gotten out of a messed-up marriage. It looks like I am in another bad one; time will tell. Time moved on and we did okay for a while. We went to play cards at my sister's house a lot. Woodrow worked long days through the week.

One morning I slept late because I was up late. Russel called me and I was half asleep, so he told me to call him back. I got up later and went to the kitchen to fix me a cup of coffee. I picked up the phone in the kitchen and hit the redial button. A woman answered the phone. I said, "I'm sorry, I must have the wrong number." I knew that a woman would not be answering Russel's phone. I thought about it for a minute and picked the phone up again and hit redial. When the lady on the other end of the phone answered, I asked her who was I speaking to? When she told me her name, I was speechless. It was Woodrow's ex-girlfriend's daughter that answered the phone. His ex-girlfriend name was Luna Lee and her daughter's name was Mila Lee. It was his ex-girlfriend daughter on the other end of the phone. This man was calling his ex-girlfriend from our home. I said to myself that I deserved better than that. When I asked Woodrow why he was calling his ex-girlfriend from the house, he lied and said he did not do it. I married another liar, congratulations to me. That was during the time he started accusing me of meeting up with some man at my sister Wilma's house. He was only trying to throw back at me he knew that was a lie. Woodrow was into so much I did not know how he kept up with it. I had been hearing rumors about him seeing someone on the east side of town. I knew not to ask him because I did not want to hear any more lies. I was told that Woodrow's truck was parked at this lady's house all the time. I let things ride on without saying a word. One Saturday, my sister, Stella, came to the house to visit. We were headed to the drug store after leaving my brother Jack's house. I wasn't aware of what street I was on until I saw Woodrow's truck at this house. I told my sister there is your brother-in-law's truck. I told her how I had been hearing about him being at this lady's house. My sister looked at me and asked me what are you getting ready to do? I said, "I'm going to stop. Stella said, "don't stop girl, let him along." We went on to the drug store.

When Woodrow got home that evening, I told him that we were not going to make it. I told him, he needed to move in the guest room. Of course, he blew up, but he knew he had no other choice.

About a couple of weeks later, he went to our pastor concerning what was going on with us. He knocked on my door one Saturday morning and asked me to go with him. I ask him where he was going? His answer was, we are going to talk to Pastor Raphael. I told him he could go but I am not going. Woodrow went to the church and talked to Pastor Raphael about what was going on. He had to have talked to the deacons as well because they sit right in front of me, and they kept turning around looking me in my face smiling. I could see him talking to Pastor Raphael, but why talk to the deacons? That really baffled me how he was handling things. He should have tried talking to pastor before he decided to do all the things he did. I found out that he was always bad mouthing me to other people. One of his cousins came to me and told me how he tried to bad mouth me to her. His cousin, Violet, is the sweetest person you would ever want to meet. He kept telling me, if he left, he wanted me to pay him out of the house. Woodrow and I separated and later got divorced. This might be hard to believe, but we get along better being divorced. I sometimes say to myself that was what we were supposed to be, just friends. Woodrow left the church and moved his membership to another church. We have continued to be friends. He have since apologized to me for everything he had done to me. I told him that I had forgiven him a long time ago. I could not have remained friends with him if I had not forgiven him. It takes a big person to say I am sorry.

After Woodrow was gone from the house for a while, someone broke in the house. I pulled up in the driveway and noticed that the side door under the carport had been broken down. I had gotten off work at seven o'clock that evening and came straight home. I was going to stop to get gas but decided to go home instead. After seeing the door had been smashed in, I backed up to the end of the driveway and called the police. While I was waiting on the police, I can see shadows in the house because my lights was shining on the house. Then this guy comes out the house with his hand in his jacket like he might have a gun. He takes offs running behind the house. There were apartment houses behind me. When the police got there, they told me to stay in the car while they go in to check the house. They came back and told me it looks like I pulled up by the time he kicked the door in, and he probably will be back since he did not succeed. I did not want to hear that. I could never understand how people feel like they can just break in and take the things you worked so hard for. I tell you I have had to put up with a lot of things, but this is crazy. It did happen again. They broke in and ram-shacked all my bedrooms. I was at work at the school this day. They stole my gun; the only protection I had. A single lady living by herself needs something. They stole all the copper out of the attic and the air condition unit out of the back yard. I was so upset that day. I got someone to put up storm doors after that. I got a storm door for the storage room to be on the safe side. I was just fed up! So many things were going through my mind at that time. By God's grace, I made it through.

I met a man about a year later that I can say for myself was a waste of time. His name was Donald. He lived in Michigan for years but was born in Mississippi. He was something else; always talking about his business he was in. Everybody in town just about had signed up under him. There were three more different businesses he had going on at the same time. The people were believing in him. I found out he was a big liar. Before you could get a question out, he already had an answer. He was always on his phone doing something. I caught him one night texting on his phone. He did not see me standing behind him, that's how deep he was into it. I mean he was texting them and waiting on responses. I stood there, I know for about two or three minutes. When I asked him what he was doing, he jumped up like the house was on fire. The expression on his face was priceless. I stopped seeing him after that. I just did not have time to be bothered with a selfish man. Of course, he called me once after I would not answer, he finally stopped calling. I literally felt like giving up on men. I think I have gone through enough.

Donald left and went back to Michigan. People were knocking on the door asking me where he was. I could not go out without someone asking me about this man. This went on for months. They just knew I knew how to get in touch with him. I just wanted to put it all behind me. I never really thought about the aftermath. I also joined his business; he had my money too.

CHAPTER

DELILAH'S SCHOOL YEARS

Being in the school system was what I liked most out of the few jobs I have had. I loved being with children and knowing that I make a difference. My daughter, Delilah, was in school also and I was able to be off when she was off. I did not have to worry about a babysitter for her. Delilah thought I was being mean when I did not let her do what the other children did. I wanted my daughter to be happy but in a safe environment. I think that speaks for most mothers. Sleepovers were something they always wanted to do. Her best friends were Chloe and Jade. Jade spent more time at my house than Chloe. They both came from a good family. Chloe grandparents and my mom and stepdad were friends. On Delilah's prom night she was so beautiful. Her date was Patrick. I think that was when Delilah started doing things that she had never done. I got her her first car when she turned sixteen. That was the first mistake. Delilah had gotten braces the year before which caused her to miss some days for her appointments. So, when the counselor sent a letter home about her missing school, I was thinking that was why. I called the counselor to let her know about the orthodontic appointments. Oh, but was I wrong! I later found out that she was out riding with Patrick on the days she should have been in school. I got a call one morning asking me why Delilah wasn't at school. So, I left work early that day so I could find out what was going on. True enough, Delilah and Patrick was at the house. I asked her why she was not at school, and she said that she was not feeling well. I knew then that I need to send her to Dreary with her dad to finish out her junior year in school. I thought I could trust her with a car of her own. I was wrong for thinking that. When I told her to pack some clothes that she was going to Dreary County where her dad was, she begged me not to send her. I knew she had to get away from Patrick right away because he was not good for her. I really wanted her to finish her senior year in Dreary County as well. Delilah did manage to finish her junior year with her dad. I let her come back home for her senior year because he was always complaining about something. Pace really did not have time for Delilah. He was too busy doing what he do. Once back to Price, I asked her why did she choose to do what she did? I will never forget the words that came out of my daughter's mouth. What she told me really did shocked me. She will never know what those words did to me. That hurt me so bad. I looked at her and told her there is a difference in scared and fear. You was not scared of me; you feared what would happen if you did not do what you were supposed to do. I told her if she did not understand now, she will one day.

Delilah finished her senior year with honors. She was always an honor student. She went on to Marsh Junior College. "Delilah had met a young man from Prescott, Mississippi that she had been dating. She came to me with him one day to tell me that she was pregnant. I asked them what their plan was, but never got a response. She started living over in Prescott with his family which I was not happy about but never said anything. She was an adult now and she made her choice. I did want her home with me. The young man's name was Demond. She later told me that he made her feel like I did not want her with me anymore. I never thought that she would ever think like that about me. I have told her many times that a person come into your life for only two reasons.

They will either be a lesson; or they will be a blessing. Delilah is married today to a young man that I am proud to call my son-in-law. His name is Maximillan, and they have five children. Two boys and three girls. My grandchildren are so precious to me. I pray that God bless and keep them healthy and happy.

CHAPTER

MEETING MY BEST FRIEND

I met my best friend in 2008. I never will forget the day I met him. I was out riding with my brother, Walter, and he stopped by his house. We started talking over the phone first, getting to know each other. He is a good person and will give you the shirt off his back. He doesn't know what the word 'no' means; always keep you laughing about something. His name is Harvey. We started going out to eat and spending more and more time together. We got along really well. He was always the same whenever you saw him. I love this man for so many reasons. When I was down, he was there for me. The people that said they would be there was no where to be found.

My vehicle broke down on me and I did not know what to do. Harvey took me to work everyday and picked me up. If he needed me today, I would go. I have been in some crazy relationships and Harvey was always there for me. He always had words of encouragements or advice. I told him that one day I was going to meet my soulmate and I hope they have a lot of his qualities. He knew me pretty well and I would never tell him that. I tell him all the time that the woman that captures his heart will be a blessed woman. He has been a blessing to me, I would not take anything for our relationship. Thank you, Harvey, for being the friend that a lot of people wish they had.

I met Malik the same year I met Harvey. Malik and I talked a lot over the phone at first because he lived in another state. He lived in Tennessee. I met him at the coffee shop where I worked at with his friend. He was passing through and decided to stop and chat with him. Baron was his friend that we worked together. If I had known then what I know now, I would have left him alone. Trust me, he was a lesson to me. He came up on weekends every now and then. Then he started talking about relocating here to Price with me. Why do everyone I meet end up wanting to move in with me. I just cannot figure that out. I let him come for a while to find a job, so he said. I made a big mistake doing that. He took his time about finding a job. He would sit and wait until I got up and went to the store, then he would call me and ask me to bring him a pace of cigarettes, a cheeseburger, and fries. Now, what if I had not gotten up to go to the store. We got into a heated argument one day because he said I went to put gas in my SUV and wouldn't put gas in his truck. I told him that I was the wrong one that he needed to be putting gas in my SUV not me putting gas in his truck. I told him that I did not know who he thought I was. If he were out trying to find a job it would be different.

When I got home from work one day, he said he had gotten a job at a warehouse in town. After a couple of months, he started complaining about hurting all the time. I have never heard him talk about ever getting his own place. He said he was not going to get paid for another two weeks. When payday rolled around, when he came in the house, he started telling me about all the people he had to pay. He then handed me a hundred-dollar bill saying that I can at least buy some things with it. I took it and threw it on the table. I looked at him and told him that those people you need to pay back haven't been furnacing him a place to stay or food to eat until you got your check. That was the end of that, I told him to leave and do not come back. He promised me that it wouldn't be like this next pay period. I did not want to hear it right then, so, he went on out the door. I do not know where he went, and I did not ask him. Before he left, he took the hundred dollars off the table. Wow!

CHAPTER

LEAVING WORK BECAUSE OF MY BACK GAVE ME TIME WITH MOM

I have been having problems with my back. I fell back in 1999 and messed up two disks in my back. My Neurosurgeon told me that I needed to have surgery, but the thought of surgery scared me. God has been good to me over the years. I was blessed to keep going until October of 2011. I tried to get up from my desk and could not move. Ms. Lydia, the teacher I worked with, got me home. I got a friend to drive me to the emergency room. That was when I started getting injections in my back and may I say, it was very painful. I wasn't able to go back to work; so, I spent a lot of time with my mom.

My mom became my brother, Pete, caregiver for several years now. Pete had some kind of episode when he got sick, and he has not been the same. Most days I would pick my mom and brother up and we would just ride. Some days we would shop, going to different stores. Mom always liked to ride, she just liked going. We were always eating out;

we did very little cooking. Every day at 5:00 p.m., I was at mom's house to watch the news with her. On this particular day, I picked my mom and brother up and I noticed that she wasn't breathing good. Mom was one you did not ask a lot of questions. I asked mom to let me take her to the emergency room. She refused saying that she will be all right. We stopped at a store that mom said she needed to run in for a minute. When mom got back in the car, I asked her again will she let me take her to the emergency room. It was something about the way she looked at me and said, "I'm going to be all right."

You did not make my mom do anything she did not want to do. It just did not rest in my spirit the way she said that. She smiled at me with the warmest smile. We watched the news but for some reason I did not want to leave mom's house that night. I left late and for some reason, I found myself riding back pass the house. I did not sleep well at all that night. When I got up my mind was on going up to mom's house, but for some strange reason it was like I had so much to do. I even went by and got my nails done that day. The red polish that I picked for my fingernails, I was anxious to show to mom. If she liked it, I was going to take her back to get hers done.

When I walked in my mom's house, I called out to her. She usually would come down the hall and say, "here I am baby." This day she did not come down the hall. I headed down the hall to her room asking her if she was going to watch the news with me. Mom was in her bed; I am still talking to her not really paying attention. I am standing there in her bedroom door saying to myself is she sleeping that hard? That was when I went over to the bed. I touched her real lightly thinking that if I shook too hard it would scare her. My mom had gone home to be with Jesus. I screamed and hollered so loud and fell to the floor. My brother was in his room in the bed asleep. I called 911 and could barely talk. I finally got the dispatcher to understand what I was saying. The dispatcher asked me if mom was breathing, and I told her no. She asked me if I could get her to the floor for CPR. I told her that she was gone and that her body was cold, and that rigor mortis had already set in. She then said, "I am sorry, and the ambulance was on the way." That was when it all hit me why I did not want to leave mom's house last night.

I was not going to see her alive anymore. I just could not stop crying. I managed to call my sister Bell and she called everybody else. The best friend I had was gone. Out of all of my mom's children, God picked me to be the one to find her. No one could have told me that I would have made it through it. No one will know how bad it hurt me. God gave me these last two years of my mom's life with her. I saw my mom practically every day. We had formed a new relationship. She often would tell me that she was going home one day. I knew that, but I just did not want her to tell me. She also told me that when we find her that she will be cold. I often wonder how did she know that? Mom was a child of God, and she lived that life where there was no question about it. She prayed for her children and her prayers is carrying me today. I miss my mom so much.

I ended up being my brother Pete's caregiver now that mom was gone. I moved back into my mom's house where he was used to being. I was going to surprise my mom by moving back home anyway. I was coming back to help her with Pete, but she transitioned home with Jesus before I made it back home.

I called all my sisters and told them my plan. I did not worry about calling the brothers because they would not have cared anyway. I did make a mistake of letting Malik come back in my life for a while. He said he had changed but he had not. He was up to his old tricks after a few months had passed. We went out to eat one evening and he stopped by to pick up his mom. His mom was a very nice lady, her name was Mrs. Horne. She had gotten an apartment and Malik was staying with her. So, after we finished our eating at the restaurant, and he gets up and leave the table saying he was going to smoke. His mom then looked at me and dropped her head. Quite naturally, somebody had to pay the ticket and I did not feel like washing dishes. You can imagine how I felt. I was too upset to speak. I paid the ticket and we left. I don't know who was the slickest him or Donald. I had no time for foolishness so, I left him along; I just wanted to be in peace.

I have some good days and some not so good since I have been my brother's caregiver. We always seemed to make it through by the grace of God. To everyone that is a caregiver, I applaud you. Everybody cannot do what we do. So, until you have walked a mile in our shoes, just don't try to judge us. Pete never complains about anything. I often wondered why no matter what job I had, I always ended up working in nursing homes and hospitals. God knew that one day I was going to be a caregiver and he prepared me for these days. I never would turn my back on teaching, I love doing both knowing at the end of the day, I made a difference in someone's life. I have had the privileged of working with some awesome teachers: Mrs. Eliana Mayes was the first teacher I worked with. She taught in Special Services. Mrs. Mayes taught me everything that I know about teaching. She was a true blessing to me. Ms. Melody Elks was the Kindergarten teacher that I worked with. She was another special person, always the same person whenever you saw her. Mrs. Ivy Norman is a very nice person once you get to know her. She teaches Social Studies. We had a rocky start, but we managed to get through it.

The injections that I was getting in my back for pain got to the point they were not doing me any good anymore. I had tried everything to keep from having surgery. I was in pain every day. I knew something had to give. I finally had the surgery done. It took me a minute, but by God's grace and mercy, I made it through. The morning after the surgery, my doctor came in the room looking for me to be in the bed. I was in the bathroom when I heard him ask the lady cleaning up the room where I was. By that time, I was coming out of the bathroom. Dr. Shaffer, my Neurosurgeon, was an awesome doctor. He gave me a thumbs up and told me that I am going to be okay if I am up and out of the bed already. My daughter stayed with me for a few days because I was having a hard time getting my feet up in the bed. I really appreciated her for that knowing that she had a family of her own to take care of. God blessed me to keep it moving by his grace and mercy. My God is an awesome God! I still hurt but not like I did before surgery. At one time, I thought I had reinjured my back, but I had not. Dr. Shaffer had an MRI done and everything was fine. He said I have a lot of arthritis that had built up but other than that, I was okay. I had to stay on the cane and back brace for a while after surgery before Dr. Shaffer told me to get rid of it. It felt so funny being free from them; I had been on that cane and brace for two years.

I started trying to work a little about two years after my back surgery. I started out doing a little sitting work. I started out working twenty hours a week; then I managed to get up to thirty after some months went by. I knew I had to get back to doing something. With the arthritis that had set up in my back, it was hard getting back in the work force. I am glad I did because I feel so much better. God's timing is not my timing; I started off having one client, then two, and three. I liked my sitting jobs, I just did not like the wear and tear on my car from all the traveling I was doing. I became very fond of my clients and did not want to leave but I had to find me something to do that did not cause me to have to travel. I am going to hang in there until I find other work.

CHAPTER

FAMILY CONVERSATIONS
AND REMEMBERING

My sister, Millie, and I, went on a cruise to Jamaica. It was my first cruise, and I was very excited about it. Being out there in all that water scared me. Millie kept telling me that I will be okay. She told me to make sure I brought some nausea medicine with me for motion sickness. When we got to, the airport, I was shocked at the lady that checked our bags. She was throwing all my lotion, bath wash, and other stuff in a waste basket. She told me that I could only have so many ounces. Millie said to me that she was in the room when I was packing but her mind was not on it to tell me that. She said to me that we will get some more later and not to worry about it.

Millie had been on cruises before, so I knew she had to not be thinking when she saw me packing it. We were supposed to have picked up some water when we landed but forgot. Millie told me how expensive everything was on the ship like water and mixed drinks.

There was a man and his wife that came on the ship the same time we did. They gave us some of their water. I really enjoyed being on that ship. One thing for sure, there was plenty of food. We went to Jamaica, The Cayman Islands, and Montego bay. There was a young man on the ship that Millie said looked like my daughter Delilah. He did look a little like her but not much to me. We took a picture together so I could show it to Delilah when we got back. I enjoyed my vacation with my sister. We did not spend a lot of time together because she lived in St. Louis. I wished that all of my sister had gone with us. My sister, Wilma, said she could not drink all that water. I used to say the same thing, but I take that all back. I will go on a cruise right now. Sometimes we need to come out of our comfort zone. I used to say I would not get on an airplane, but I am over those days. I like traveling. When you drive you can see more. I wanted to book another cruise right after we got back. I did not want to come back so soon.

Every Easter weekend, we have a family celebration weekend in remembrance of mom. Every year we had a birthday party for mom; so, we said we would celebrate on Easter weekend because it was a four-day weekend. If everyone made it by that Friday night, we would do a fish fry and Saturday was always bar-b-que day. Sundays we would finish off everything from Saturday's bar-b-que. Everyone was headed back home on Monday. It's Always good to see the whole family come together once a year. I made sure and so did everyone else made sure that we kept that weekend open.

One year my niece, Skylar, rented a place downtown for the celebration. It was a very nice place but not big enough. When you get everyone together in one place it tends to get a little crowded. Despite of it all, we all had a nice time. There is always somebody that is going to complain that is just the way people are. Family is supposed to just be glad to be together. It all worked out in the end. Everyone had a wonderful time.

This makes me think of the time I left my home church and started attending another church. I knew my mom did not like it when I left but she did not say anything. It is really sad to say but I can not remember why I left. All I know is it had to be bad enough for me to have left. I would sometimes come by the house to see mom after church. I asked her one day to come and go with me to church one Sunday. That is when she let me have it. I never will forget that day as long as I live. Mom looked at me and said if she went to church it would be her own church. She told me to stop going to other churches when I needed to be at my own church. I just stood there with my eyes bucked. Mom had been quiet long enough, I guess. She said that every church has problems that I could not do anything about that. She then tells me to go back to my own church and do what you are supposed to do, and don't worry about what other people are doing. Mom said to me, "baby, you have got to seek your own soul salvation." God is the one to do the chastising. My mom was a very wise lady.

I did go back after my mom transitioned. Her words to me is what has kept me in so many ways. Right after that, I joined back at my home church. Something was said that really upset me, but I remember mom's words and I shoved it of my shoulders. "Thank God for mom, y'all!"

I finally got my brother, Pete, in an adult daycare. That was a big help to me. It gave me some time to myself. The problem came in when the home health agency sent out someone to give him a shower and a shave. Lord, they sent a lady, and he had a fit. He had the lady standing outside the bathroom door asking him to open the door. I felt so bad for her. I told her I was hoping he was not going to act like that. They ended up sending a man after a month or so. It was my classmate, Purvis. He had been working for the company for years. Purvis was dating my best friend Tracey in high school. The three of us were best friends. Purvis did not marry Tracey; instead, he married another classmate, Ivory. Everything was going good; Pete liked Purvis. We later changed companies and we could not keep Purvis. He was the only orderly that worked for his company. The other company did not have any orderlies. To be honest, you just could not find men much working for home health agencies. I took over for a while doing what I could and later my daughter, Delilah, started helping us out. I sure do miss having Purvis around.

My nephew and his wife, Melanie, got married in Florida on the beach. It was a beautiful wedding. I made the biggest mistake of my life by inviting Crayton Waton to go with me. First of all, he did not want to get a hotel room. Second, he complained about having to get dressed in my sister's hotel room. I got my brother, Pete, ready first, and he went on with my sisters Clara and Ashley. Crayton started complaining so much he was getting on my nerves. He did not want to go into the reception to at least speak to everyone. He wanted to get back on the road going back to Price. I was so fed up with him; I did not blame anybody but myself for bringing him. May I say that I got back on the road. There were no words said on the way back. The only words I spoke was to Pete. When I got back home, I took him to his house, and I came back to mine. I promised myself that I would never take him anywhere with me. He would have probably acted the same if we were in Canada. I just kept praying asking God to make my niece and nephew understand. To know that it was not me but the company I was keeping. I got a call from my sisters asking me if everything was alright. It was so embarrassing. I am so glad I saw the real him before I married him. A month before Crayton and I was supposed to have gotten married, I woke up one morning, sat straight up in the bed. I said, "I can't do it, I can't marry this man." Since we had already had counseling with my pastor, I called him first. Time pastor said hello, the first words out of my mouth was, "I can't do it." Pastor asked me what was wrong, and I told him that I can not marry that man. He told me that whatever decision I made, that he would support me. I thanked my pastor and hung up the phone. I then called Crayton and told him. The first thing he did was start lecturing me saying how I was wrong for doing this. He started saying things like how good he had been to me. I told him that I was not going to argue with him, I wish him the best. I told him that he could get his rings back. He said to me that he bought those rings for me. He has not spoken to me since. I have seen him out from time to time and he would stare at me. His daughter and I see each other sometimes out in the stores or somewhere. Her name is Evenlyn, and she is the sweetest person. Always the same; I don't care where you see her.

My two sisters, Ashley and Clara, along with my two nieces, Leah and Charlotte, and my nephew, Peterson, went on a much-needed vacation. We went on a cruise to Belize, the Cayman Islands, Jamaica and Mahogany Bay. We had a wonderful time; we did some of everything. At the captain's dinner, we all dressed up. We went snorkeling to see the dolphins at the aquarium. There were many shows, Karaoke and so much more. The shopping was awesome. I was so afraid I would not have enough room to bring everything back. There were many pictures taken of the ship and the places we stopped at like restaurants, especially the dolphins. We met a nice couple that sat at the table with us. Their names were Marshall and Emily. We ended up doing a lot of stuff together. They were a really down to earth couple. We have stayed in touch over social media. I don't remember what state they were from. I really appreciated my sister, Stell and her husband, for letting my brother Pete stay with them while I was gone. I was a better person when I got back. You never really know how bad you need a vacation until you take one. When we got back, we were making plans to go somewhere else.

We have taken many trips to Biloxi, Mississippi. There was one year when we spent the fourth of July down there. There was a mix up one time when everyone was supposed to be in Biloxi. Clara and Ashley ended up on the Gulf Shores in Alabama. I have never been over that far, but I hear that it is nice. For more reason or another, we could never all be in the same place at the same time. Those brothers were not particularly concerned it wasn't something they though twice about. All the sisters did end up together the Christmas we rented a cabin in Blue Ridge Mountains in Tennessee. We had an awesome time. The bears I never saw, but I did hear about how they would tear the trash up. Those curves going up and down those mountains were so scary; you could look down on the roof of the cabins. I was so amazed at how high the hills were. Once I got up to the cabin, I did not go back down for anything until it was time to go. My nieces went down to the store, they did not pay attention to things like that.

We usually would order t-shirts for the family celebration but this year we decided we were going to buy yellow t-shirts. It did not work out good at all. There were yellow and neon green. That was the first year we all had on different colors. So, now we have decided on sticking with ordering more shirts every year or wearing the ones we already have. We all still had a goodtime, everybody was home that year. Scattered at the store, visiting other people just everywhere. We went on to take pictures of the ones that was there in one place.

My nephews, Noland and Ethan, are the two that would take care of the meat and the grilling. Ethan usually grilled the most. These two knew how to get things done. We are from my niece Skylar's house to the home house where Pete and I are. Skylar would get someone she knew to cater most of the food. I have really appreciated my niece and nephews over the years for taking a load off me. The next year, we were all in the same color t-shirt because they were ordered from the same t-shirt person we always used.

Out of all the times I really needed to get away for a few days, I had gotten a promotion for a cruise about a month before. I called my sister Clara, and we booked that cruise. My sister Ashley, and my nieces Skylar, and Charlotte went as well. I have always been the kind of person that love sharing good things with my family and friends. Life is about the choices that you make. My choice is to be a better person each day. We took this cruise the first part of July, so, everywhere you looked you saw red, white and blue. Everything was really nice. The restaurant that we went to in downtown Ft. Lauderdale had a live band outside and you could eat inside or outside. We chose to eat outside to hear the band and watch people walking to and fro. The traffic was very busy, and our table was right near the sidewalk. My niece Skylar had a Cowboys purse that I really like, if it had the San Francisco 49ers on it. We all needed that vacation and we enjoyed it. I like cruises that last for several days. One thing about going on one is you always end up with almost as much or more stuff from shopping than what you bring with you on the trip. This was the last cruise we went on in July of 2018. Time is so valuable, don't put off for tomorrow what you can do today. I thank God for allowing me to think like that. I still wished that all my sisters could have taken that cruise or the ones before.

My sister Clara called me one weekend and said she had gotten a couple of flights to Las Vegas. I had never been to Las Vegas but have heard a lot about it. It was a beautiful sight flying into Vegas that night. I was told that they always flew in at night because of the scenery. That was a wise choice. When we got to our hotel, we could not stop being excited about everything we were seeing. They were right about this being a city where no one sleeps. I did not care what time you got up; people were everywhere.

Our first day there, we got on a bus that took us downtown to the different buildings. We were from one building to the next. My sister can really walk. It was so hot you could smell the heat in your nose. I don't ever want to go back when it is hot. I was so glad to get back to the hotel for a shower. Everyone kept telling us to stay hydrated, but you did not have any choice. I drank water like an elephant. Clara said we was not going to walk too much the next day. It seemed like I walked more the next day than the day before. It was a lot to see despite the heat. They had buses that came through every fifteen minutes. There was no way you got left anywhere. We took a tour at night so we could really see all the beauty of Las Vegas at night. The day we went shopping there was a mixed drink stand and we got some frozen mixed drinks. We shopped and enjoyed going from store to store. But it seemed like that frozen mixed drink had me so thirsty it was like I wanted to drink a gallon of water. Let me be the one to tell you to not drink any alcoholic beverages while you are outside and keep water with you, I don't care what. I saw so many Elvis impersonators. There were many bands that all you had to do was just stop and enjoy. While you are shopping, you can hear them playing while you shop. It was a really nice trip; we enjoyed ourselves. Remember to bring your walking shoes. I saw people driving but did not see how they got through all the crowds without constantly stopping. It is better to walk and take the buses. Now that is just my opinion. If you are going to walk, bring your walking shoes for sure, if you are going with someone like Clara who don't mind walking. I mentioned to Clara that we should go back when the weather is cooler.

FAMILY TRANSITIONS

My brother Russel's son, Russel, Jr. and his family came down to see him. I had not seen Pete Jr. since he was maybe four or five. He is now a grown man with a family of his own. I was so happy to see that they finally came together after so many years. The break-up between Russel Jr.'s mom and my brother got better somewhat because Russel told me how they would talk from time to time. Right after they got together, Russel started getting sick and was in and out of the hospital. Russel Jr. asked him if he wanted to come to Pennsylvania where he was. Russel told him he was going to stay at home. Russel and I talked everyday no matter what. I would sometimes go by and sit with him and his wife Oliva. When I cooked something, I would always think about them. I would fix plates and take it to them or if Russel was out, he would come by and pick it up.

There were times when he would call and I was not able to answer, he would leave a voice mail saying this is your brother Russel; I repeat this is your brother Russel, call me when you get a chance. I wished I had kept that last voice mail. The time Russel went in the hospital he did not make it back home. Russel transitioned home to be with Jesus. That was a sad day for the family. I don't think anyone was expecting him to be gone.

Russel was always the life of any party. He could tell you some jokes that made you laugh and laugh. I miss him so much. I erased that last voice mail about two weeks before he transitioned home. If I had not erased it, I cold at least hear his voice when I played the voicemail back. I guess it is for the best; it would have only made me cry. We loved him but God loved him more. I have managed to keep in touch with Russel's wife Olivia for a while but due to circumstances, we don't communicate like we used to. Olivia will always be my sister-n-law, no matter what.

My sister Millie and I talked every day. We would talk for hours and hours at a time. Sometimes we would ask each other what time it was and laughed. This lady here, when it came to working, we were just alike. We believed in working for what we wanted. When I was not on the phone with her, I was usually on the phone with Russel. We all have our ways that is just a part of life. Love will hide a multitude of faults. One thing about my family is, we might disagree with each other at times, but love has kept us together. Millie and I would disagree to agree, but always told each other I love you before we got off the phone.

Millie, Clara, and Ashley all lived in St. Louis. I have been to St. Louis so many times, you would have thought I lived there at one time. My sister asked me many times to move there, but St. Louis was a little too fast for me. Millie got sick and did not do good for a while, but she eventually was okay.

Times when I would visit, we all would end up at Clara's house and what a beautiful house. She had her house built just the way she wanted it. There have been so many good times spent at Clara's house. My brother Pete and I loved visiting St. Louis. Ashley and Millie was mostly at Clara's house when we were there, but we enjoyed the times at their house too. We just couldn't find enough things to do, we were all over the place.

During the Christmas holiday, Clara decorate her house so beautifully. She has a high ceiling and always have a tree that stand so tall; it's really something to see. Millie and her three daughters went on a cruise they said they really enjoyed. Millie's three daughters are Penelope, Autumn, and Camila. They have a brother Owen that would not have cared about going on a cruise. He is a hard-working young man, and his mom says that God has a plan for his life. A mother will always pray for her children and my sister did. As time passed, I noticed that the conversations on the phone with Millie got shorter and shorter. I never asked any questions; I just went by what she told me. I recalled times when she would say that she was going to take a nap. I have never known her to take a nap in the middle of the day. She decided to tell me that she was sick again, that she had been to the doctor. We talked for a long time that day. I stayed in prayer that God would direct the doctor as to what was best for her. I never in a million years thought that she was getting ready to transition from this world. If I had known, I would have spent more time with her. The last thing she said to me was how she missed the long conversations that we used to have. I hugged her and told her that we will be together again one day and have those long conversations again. I was hurting for my nieces and nephew as well. This has been a long year for the family. We have lost a brother and a sister in the same year. "Lord have mercy!"

It was really hard for me to get myself together for a while. God has blessed me to keep it moving. I don't care what no one says, but it is a different feeling losing each family member There is a different hurt with each transition. I said to myself that I need to get away somewhere. I felt like I wanted to just go off by myself and just soak in my feelings. I did not do it because I realized I did not need to do that; God does not make any mistakes. We just have to learn to live with it. It doesn't stop it from hurting. We did manage to go to Biloxi, Mississippi for a few days. My sisters, Ashley, and Clara along with my brother Pete, and myself. We just felt like getting away. We took a tour of Biloxi and went to the place where they had everyone's name on a wall that died during Hurricane Katrina. There are many places there that have some sort of history behind it. It is really something to see especially if you love history like I do. It did help me some to go on that vacation, but I still had a long way to go. I have caught myself picking up the phone to call Millie. Then I would say to myself that she has gone home to be with Jesus. When I tell you that we talked every day, I mean every day.

CHAPTER

GOING BACK TO WORK AT JEFFERSON MIDDLE SCHOOL

I continued to do sitting work until I said I was going to go talk with the principal at the elementary school. I was not sure if I wanted to stop at the elementary school two houses from me or keep going out east of town to Jefferson Middle School. I ended up at Jefferson Middle School. While I was standing there talking to the secretary about job openings there when Mr. Monroe came in. I had not seen him since I had to leave my job at the school in 2011. Mr. Monroe was a good person and was always there for his employees. We greeted each other and I asked him if he had a job for me. I was blessed that day because he did have a job opening. Mr. Monroe told me that he was going to get back with me before that day was out. He did call me back that day to tell me, Welcome Aboard. I was back in the classroom again, where I love being with my students. I would not have wanted to be anywhere else. Satan stayed on my track that year. I had to ask God for strength to keep going on some of those days. I do know that if you live in this life, trouble will come.

Walking into the doors of Jefferson Middle School felt good. It was not about me, it was about the children, nothing else is important. I feel like this, I am going to do my job just make sure you do yours. We are all grown, and we are all in this thing together.

This teacher was new in the teaching field which I understood. Her name was Mrs. Duncan who is the first teacher that I could not get along with. She and I have had some trying times. I have never had a problem working with anyone, I mean never. When I mentioned it to people that I knew and have worked with, they looked at me in dismay. They would say really not you, you can get along with anybody. My response was always, "My thoughts exactly." I thank God for my co-worker, Mrs. Wallace, she helped me through a lot of things that year. I appreciate you, Mrs. Wallace. There was one other teacher at Jefferson Middle School that played a big part in that school year. Ms. Penn talked to me and prayed a lot for me. Thank you for your prayers and the talks we had. I pray that God continue to bless and keep you. Mrs. Duncan and I worked through our difficulties. She is really not a bad person; she has come a long way with her approach. I pray that we will have a better year next year.

We went on a much-needed vacation to Biloxi, MS. I tell you I was so ready to get this time away. We stayed for a few days doing our usual things. The beach was hot, but we still enjoyed. One of my friend ladies got married in July. She had a beautiful wedding and I told her she will never look that pretty again. She was a beautiful bride. She has forever wanted me to come work with her; her name is Brooklyn. Brooklyn is a real estate broker. It looks so easy for her because she has been doing this for years. I told her to leave me where I am best at doing and that is in the classroom with my children. She never lets up, no matter what I say to her. You can not help but love her. Before summer was over, the family decided to get together at the home house for a bar-b-que. My nephews Noland, and Ethan, were ready because that was their specialties. The ladies did all the sides. Ethan and the brothers liked playing Domino's and the ladies mostly played Spade of Whiz. I was always better at Spade than I was at Whiz. I could never keep in my head that Spades was not always trunk when you played Whiz. We sometimes played deuces is wild for a quarter. I sometimes wonder what happen to the simpler games we played that was so much fun like Uno, Scrabble, Checkers and Twister. I remember having lots of fun with those games. There is nothing wrong with the old-time way. Hey, it's what we were brought up on. If it was good enough then, it should be good enough now. My most enjoyable times with my family is when we would all sit around and talk about the good old days. Looking back on those days it seemed like things were simpler then, and it did not take much to have fun.

By this point in my life, I am in my comfort zone when it comes to relationships. You remember me telling you about Perez? Perez would text me from time to time to see how I was doing. I have only saw him maybe once or twice since college. We started chatting over the phone every now and then. The first conversation I had with him was not impressive to me at all. I am asking myself why was he talking like he was all that? I thought that maybe he was trying to see my reaction to how he was talking. But then there was another conversation then another and that was when I said that he was arrogant.

I know that I could never be the woman for him. I am the kind of person that say very little but observe a lot. I will take all I can and then I am gone. It was always 'I need you to do this or that.' He was the only one that knew how to do things right. Sometimes we can be our own worst enemy. The times when I would tell him about himself, he would just laugh. Perez acted as if people owed him something. When we talked about our school days, we always had fun. I have yet to hear an apology of any kind come out of his mouth. We all have our faults, but some are so much worst than others. I pray that Perez find his happiness someday. One day maybe we will be able to sit down and have a decent conversation. I have been by myself for the last five years and like I said earlier, I am in my comfort zone.

CHAPTER

SUMMER IS OVER AND MY
GUARD IS DOWN AGAIN

School is back in session. The students were excited, and we were
excited to see them. The school year was off to a good start. I went
into the school year with the determination that it was going to be a
good year. Before we knew it, we were decorating for Halloween. I had
met someone online whom I knew from years ago. He said everything
that I wanted to hear. He said he was a man of God, and that God
came first in his life. I found out that it was not true at all. After a few
weeks of being around him, the whole picture was clear as if I had
drawn it myself. His name was Dean. I texted him back and told him
I was headed to Krogers. He texted and asked me to pick him up, and
what did he do that for. I texted him back and told him, no. That was
when he decided to pick up the phone and call. He asked me what was
wrong? I told him he was not the kind of man that I needed in my life.
He wanted to know what he had done, and I asked him was he really

asking me that question. I had been by myself for five years and let my guard down again because of the way he led me to believe that he was a good man. People really need to stop lying with God. He swore over and over again that I was the woman that he has been praying for. I told him that the woman he has been praying for is not me. God's word say to be ye equally yoked together and believe me we are not that at all. It took me a while to get him to understand that, but I think he does now. I am a peaceful person and I live a peaceful life. My brother Pete and I will be just find by the grace of God. If it takes another five years for me to spend alone, so let it be. I pray that he find the woman he deserves to be with. Dean would have been a person that I would have kept as a friend, but he did not want that.

I guess by me being by myself for five years, I was lonely and needed somebody to fill that void in my life. I realized that now and pray every day that the next time I let someone into my life that it is in God's will. Sometimes we just have to be still and wait. God's timing is not our timing besides, I am good now, I am back in my comfort zone. Maybe one day in the near future, things will change. I am trusting in God! Besides, I need to get to know me. Happiness is so important; I would rather be by myself and happy than to be in a relationship that I am miserable in. It's been said that a piece of a man is better than no man at all. That's a lie from the pits of hell! I have made many bad choices in my life and own up to that, but I always knew how to walk away when things was not right. People come into your life for two reasons. They will either be a lesson or a blessing. I can say that I have been taught many lessons in my life.

My students were so excited when we got ready to decorate the pumpkins and decorate the door. Mrs. Wallace was the one that did all the decorating. We called her the artist in the room, and she had so many great ideas. The children enjoyed there Halloween especially their trick-or-treat bag that they got. We made sure that they did not eat too much sugar for us as well as their parents. We all knew what sugar do to kids. When we got back that Monday morning it was time to start decorating for Thanksgiving. The children loved having a part in the decorating. In the next three weeks, we will be out enjoying our families and friends. I have spent the last five Thanksgivings alone with just Pete and me and we have survived. We will survive this year also. It just feel so different when you don't have that significant other. I cannot help but think of how I am going to spend Christmas. I'll just have to wait and see; Thanksgiving has not gotten here yet.

The employees at Jefferson Middle School did a dinner, everyone brought something. We had a little something in the room for the children. That the only thing about the holidays is how much I miss the children. I can remember the time when Thanksgiving was a special holiday when all the family got together to enjoy each other. Now we look over Thanksgiving to Christmas. When Thanksgiving comes around the Christmas trees are already up in the stores and most homes. It was so different when I was a little girl. The neighbors all cooked along with my mom and everybody in the neighborhood got together and had so much fun and you could feel the love. I pray that my students will have a good and enjoyable holiday.

CHAPTER

THE YEAR 2019

I spent the holiday doing absolutely nothing. My niece, Skylar, did Thanksgiving at her house which was a blessing because I did not feel like cooking. She had food from one corner of the room to the next. We really enjoyed everything. Thank you so much, Skylar. I am planning on Pete and myself being in St. Louis with Clara and Ashley for Christmas Thanksgiving went by so fast. You never know how much you need a break until you get one. It will be time to get back to the classroom on Monday.

It was so good to see my students. Everyone looked happy and healthy. We talked about what everyone did over the holidays, and everyone was very talkative. Now it's time to get back to work. We have about three weeks before we are out again for Christmas. It was hard getting students to focus because the biggest holiday for them is Christmas. Everyone finally settled down and learning began. There was work that had to be prepared for them to take home over the holidays also.

I remember when I found out that there was no Santa Claus. Every Christmas Eve night my two older sisters, Wilma and Stella, was always able to stay up but the younger children had to go to bed. Mom would always say that Santa Claus won't come until we went to sleep. I asked my mom how it is that Wilma and Stella can stay up and I couldn't and that's when mom told me. She said you were always nosy, weren't you? Time daybreak would hit we were up riding our bikes and skating up and down the street. Our friends were out also, and we would talk about everything we got for Christmas. I have been through a lot of Christmas holidays, but it is still the most exciting time of the year. We decorated the room and that really made it feel like Christmas was in the air. Do anyone believe in Christmas miracles anymore? I know that I still do and every year I pray for one. It might not come this year, but I am not going to give up. I would like to spend Christmas somewhere where there is snow. That would make it seem more like Christmas, it is something I have always dreamed of. It would also be nice to spend New Year's there too. It was time for me to say goodbye to my students again. It will be another year when we see each other again. I pray that they have the best Christmas ever and to stay healthy, happy and to get everything they wanted for Christmas.

Shopping for loved ones for Christmas has always been something that I never liked doing because you never know what to get them. I wished I could take each one to pick out their own Christmas present. But I know that it would not be the same as taking out time to pick one out for them. Somehow, I always managed to get through it. I am a last-minute shopper. When I say last minute, I am usually shopping Christmas Eve. Christmas was like it has been every year when it comes to having that special person in my life. Pete and I did spend the holidays in St. Louis. My sister, Clara, always out-do herself for the holidays with all the cooking. There was a lot of eating at that house over the holidays. I really enjoyed our Christmas break. For New Year's, I stayed home and cooked black-eyed peas, cabbage, bar-b-que and corn bread. I would always buy a cake or pie. Sometimes I would go to a family member's house for desserts. If I could only have another week off, it would be awesome. You don't know how much you enjoy being off until you are off. I was missing my children at school so it's time to go back on Monday.

It was good to see the children all back to school. They had so much to tell us about their Christmas break. We let them get it all out the first day back, but it was different the next day. I was back to work for us. I don't know what was going on when we got back to school, but I had this urge to sanitize and clean every day. I kept saying to Mrs. Wallace to sanitize her area too. She asked me what was going on and I told her I did not know but it was like a lot of germs in the air. I told Mrs. Wallace that I could just feel it. I could not explain what was going on with me. I do know now that it was the Spirit of the Lord. From January until Spring Break in March, I never let up with sanitizing every time I got to work. About three days into Spring break the media started talking about the Corona Virus(Covid-19). We were supposed to have been out for a week and it never happened. My birthday was the weekend after we got out and I could not do anything. They got the first case of Covid-19 here in Mississippi on my birthday, wow! That was the first year I did nothing for my birthday. My plans were to go to Memphis, Tennessee. My plans were not God's plan. I was not disappointed bout it, but I knew it was for the best. The pandemic took the world by storm. Everything shut down. Restaurants, churches, barber shops, salons; I mean everything. I have never had a problem with staying at home, just not like this. We ended up going back in May to stack everything out of the way so that maintenance could sanitize and deep clean the building. We got everything we needed out of the classroom. This enemy, Covid-19, has killed a lot of people. We could not go back for the rest of the year.

This year began with virtual learning. We spent the first part of the year making sure that all the students had computers and a hot spot to get online. It was not so bad starting off, we had awesome parents. With their help, we had a good year. I missed having the children in the classroom, but it was all we could do with this virus being so out-of-hand. We have the best student; we could not have asked for better. By the time I thought everything was off to a good start, Mrs. Wallace had put in for her retirement. I was so shocked! She had said that it would be later on in the year before she left but changed her mind. I was hoping she would finish out the whole school year. When I thought about it, I really did not blame her. She has been a very dedicated worker for Price Public School District for years. We worked well together and got along well too. Mrs. Wallace is a very nice person, everybody loved her. My niece, Ivy, was in her room and she just loved here. So that left me and Mrs. Duncan. Since we were virtual, we did not get anyone else to replace her.

Mrs. Duncan and I were saying if we could get a young man to work with us that would be good. We both knew that was a big if. It just was not the same feeling teaching the children online as having them in the classroom. Then it got to the point we were not allowed to send goody bags or anything home. We always made sure that they knew that we loved them. It made me wanting to send money every holiday or birthday. I can not wait until we can all get back together. When they started saying that they were coming out with a vaccine for the Covid-19, most people was saying they were not going to take it. I said I am going to take it because I have that kind of faith. I made sure that my brother Pete and I got fully vaccinated and I am glad we did. I think about eighty percent of my family is fully vaccinated also. I do not judge those that have not been vaccinated, we all have our reasons.

The months went by pretty fast that year. It was Thanksgiving already. I usually would have gone to St. Louis but we were waking up to 1,600 to 1,700 cases a day. I spent a quiet lazy day at home for Thanksgiving. Pete and I got full of dressing, potato salad, greens, cake and pie. We were doing just dandy. No one was visiting much these days. The phones are the best thing going now. I have got to do what I need to do to keep safe and so is everyone else. This pandemic has changed everyone's life. Life will probably never be the same, we will all have a new way of living. Christmas is only a few weeks away and so many places to shop has closed their doors.

There is something about the Christmas holidays that is different being by yourself other than any other holiday for me. My brother Russel always had a saying that it is what it is. I miss Russel, he was always saying things to make you look at him twice. He was one that knew how to make you laugh. Russel was a very outgoing person. He like to make things happen. I know this year my brother Pete and I will be spending Christmas at home. They are asking people to stay home and not travel. Of course, no one listened to that; they traveled anyway. They are saying that there will be another surge during these two big holidays, Christmas and New Year's. I guess some people are going to do what they want to do in spite of.

With the Covid-19 surge getting so bad, we worked from home the last week before Christmas break. I am praying that the vaccine that they have will be the beginning to the end of this nightmare. I have been going out to get what I needed and back to the house. Someone asked me how is it that a person with so much faith be afraid of getting the virus? My response was, first of all, God gave me five senses and he wants me to use them. I think people really need to think before they speak. I have turned a deaf ear to a lot of this nonsense.

My grandchildren send me a list every year. The older they get the longer it gets. I prayed I could get everything in one day. It would be really nice if I could get everything in one store. There is only six days left before Christmas and I was ready to be finished shopping already. The long lines is another thing. I get worn out just standing in line. I thank God that he allowed me to see another Christmas season. I prayed for the families that has lost loved ones as I do every day. This is the first Christmas since the pandemic started, and there have been a lot of lives lost. People always say that time will heal, but I think that time make it better. Time will heal some things, but not all. The pain will get better in time. I do pray for our children to have some kind of Christmas.

It was always hard going back to work after Christmas break January 2021. I can get spoiled easily by sleeping late and doing nothing all day. After a week back, I am usually good. The children was geared up and ready to go. Time went by pretty fast, but we stayed on course. When spring break came that year Pete and I had decided we were not going anywhere. Pete has gotten to the point where he did not want to go at all. He has been going to the bathroom a lot more than usual. You never really know because he never complain about anything. Every time I would ask him if he was okay, he would say yes. He could not be okay from what I could see. A week after we got back from spring break, I took him to the doctor. The medicine that he doctor put him on seem to help a little, but there was something not quite right with him.

This school year has been real challenging for the teacher as well as the students. We do what we have to do to help our students learn. I can not see myself being around them and not hug them and show love. The end of the year was fast approaching. The children are supposed to be back in the classroom next school term. Everyone is looking forward to the summer break. Mr. Monroe our principal nor our assistant principal, will not be here next year. We hate to lose the best principal and the best assistant principal in the world. I do not know who we are getting to replace them. I do know that God is large and in charge. I am going to miss seeing them next school term. It is now April, and we are getting everything together to make sure that our student will have something that they can work on during the summer months. Just something to make sure they don't lose what they have learned over the school year. Mrs. Duncan is the one who get everything prepared for them. She is always making sure that they have something to do. We sure did miss having Mrs. Wallace in the class with us this year. I know she probably is enjoying her retirement being able to enjoy her children and grandchildren. I used to tell her all the time that I was going to grow up and be just like her.

Pete ended up in the hospital after I saw that he was not doing any better I took him to the hospital. When we got there, they started asking questions. I answered to the best of my ability because Pete can't get his sentences out like he use to. I was thinking that we would be out at the end of the day, but it ended up being days. I was not looking for us to be there from April 29th to May 21st. I had to do what I had to do. Those couches at that hospital was the hardest I have ever tried to sleep on, but I made it. I do not ever want to go through that again, I was really miserable. The staff were the best. They gave me plenty of covers trying to make me more comfortable. I thank them for everything that they did for us. I was just taking one day at a time. I did not make it back to school for the end of the year. Pete needed me right now more than he ever have. I remember my mom saying to me that if something was to happen to her that she was leaving enough of us behind to take care of each other. I have experienced a totally different thing since she has been gone. She would always also say that "I did not raise y'all like that, I raised y'all to love one another and to take care of each other." I sit sometimes and just cry because I miss being able to talk to my mom. I often pray that God will intervene and let everyone see what it is that we are doing. There is one thing I do know and that is God sees and he cares. I am so glad that God has given me the spirit of forgiveness. Holding things inside I have learned will consume you. It is not about what people do to me, but about what I do to them. I want to live a happy life because time is so valuable. There are some people that think they are always right, and you are wrong. Those kinds of people make me tired just listening to them. When things don't go their way, they get upset and won't come around. They really are not conscious of the things that they do. I can not talk much about that it makes me sad, I am sure there are some of these types of people in every family. We all know that no one is perfect, we all have our faults, but we can do better. There is nothing wrong with admitting that you are wrong and saying I am sorry. It take a big person to tell someone those two words. There are times when I would say that if there is anything that I said or done to anyone, I am sorry.

I hated not being able to see the children before they left for summer break. I prayed for them to have a happy and safe summer. I know some of them will be traveling visiting family and so forth. I am thinking back on my summer vacations, and I do not remember traveling out of state with my parents. Maybe because it was so many of us. My mom and stepdad travelled out of state. Mom had an uncle in Pennsylvania. She told me one day how he kept asking her to let him raise some of her children. Mom's uncle name was Phillip. She said that they needed to stay together. I travelled to Pennsylvania with mom and my sister Bell. I drove all the way there and all the way back with two drivers in the car. I could not get either one of them to drive. Sometimes I wonder what it would have been like to live in another state being raised in Pennsylvania. I know that a lot of families travel during the summer, and I pray for there safe return. Summer vacation go by so quickly when you are having fun.

Unfortunately, I was not able to return to work at Jefferson School District. I do not have anyone that my brother Pete can stay with until

I work. The daycare has not opened back up yet. I am not sure if he need to with this virus spiking up again. I was really looking forward to seeing the children in person this year. I am going to really miss them. My brother Pete is my main focus right now. It is going to be challenging but I can do it. I can do all things through Christ who strengthens me. I have been fortunate to have had my sister Wilma to help me for a year while I worked. This time at home will give me a chance to do some of the things I have wanted to do. Finishing the book that I am writing will be one of those things. You know it would be really nice if the school district had a child daycare and an adult daycare. That is just wishful thinking I know, but it is a thought. I do have a lot to do at the house too. I have heard many times from ladies that I know that there is nothing to do at home. I have yet to see that. There is always something to do at the house, the thing of it is if you want to do it. I know one thing for sure it is so easy to get spoiled from sleeping late. I cannot get in that mode because it makes me lazy when I am used to my feet hitting the floor at four-thirty every morning. The times that I have slept late, I woke up with a headache. I don't know why that is, maybe it is psychological. I am getting close to retirement age, and I need to learn to relax more and sleep late. I have gotten the carport closed in and had concrete poured for the extra driveway. I got my sign finally hung outside. I am getting things done little by little. Oh yes, I finally found the bricks I wanted to go around my flower bed. Like I said, there is always something to do at home. I thank God that he blesses me to get it done.

I have visited a lot of places in my lifetime but there are so many more I want to see. I am praying that one day in the near future that I will. One of my biggest dreams is to fly over the Golden Gate Bridge of San Francisco. I want to then drive across it. I want it to be at night when I fly over the Golden Gate Bridge so I can really see the beauty of it from the sky. I also want to visit Niagara Falls from the state side and Canada side and the snow capped mountains of Colorado. Then there is Minnesota, Washington, DC, Arizona, Oklahoma, Nebraska, Utah, Wyoming, Rhode Island, Maine, Pennsylvania and of course, Hawaii and Paris. All the states I have not visited. It would really be nice to travel by car to some of them to be able to see more. I have had people to tell me that there is no way I will be able to visit all those states and I would always say that with God all things are possible. My sister Millie also wanted to do a lot of traveling we had planned on traveling together before she transitioned. Millie talked about buying an RV to travel the country in. I was going to be right there with her. An RV is the ideal thing to travel in. I love you Millie, but God loved you more.

I have always like going and have always wanted to visit other places to see how other people lived and do things. I am the same way about visiting other churches. I know I have been talked about because of that. It is not that I am not satisfied with my church because we are family. I just never saw a problem with it. I have always been an outspoken person, if you ask me my opinion, I will definitely give it to you. We are all entitled to that am I right? Back to traveling the world. I know that there are many of you that is looking forward to traveling as well.

I have always lived in Mississippi. I would love to experience living somewhere else just to try it for a few years. I was going to move to St. Louis where my youngest sisters live. I think St. Louis is a little too fast pace for me. I really thought about it after my mom transitioned home with Jesus. But having my oldest brother Pete to think of too, has kept me in one place. It's been almost ten years and about five months. I was ten years younger when mom transitioned, now I am ten years older. I have never wanted to go North to live but did think of moving north to Tennessee. Then there are times when I feel like it was meant for me to stay here. If it's meant for me to move, I will. That is why I have said that life is full of the choices we make. That is why I always say don't do things and blame other people when things don't turn out the way you wanted it to. No one can make a decision on your life. I am comfortable where I am here at home. It is just that little something that stays with me for some reason. Do you ever sometimes feel like uprooting and moving somewhere out of state? I am going to say what my brother Russel would say if he was here, "it is what it is." I miss having you here Russel.

I AM REALLY A COUNTRY GIRL AT HEART

When I was a little girl, I loved going to my big mama house. I have never really liked living in the city. If I could take this house and move it to the country, it would make me so happy. They used to move houses at one time, I don't think they do it anymore. If this was not the family home which is my mom's house I probably would have been in the country. The air is so much fresher also. I probably would have the biggest garden you would ever want to see. I used to have this dream of moving to the country buying a lot of land and horses. I dreamed of a riding trail and a big recreational place with tennis, basketball, skating, bike riding and much more for families to come to on the weekends.

My whole focus would be on the children and giving them something to look forward to. I have always wanted to have something for the children, all children. It is all about the children. I had that dream for years. It still would be nice to do. I thought about what did we have to do on weekends out of school. The only thing I could think of was the football games on Friday nights. Be for real now we had nothing to do. We need something for our kids. I just wished that I had a few others that would agree and invest with me to make things happen. You have got to love the country y'all.

Time waits on no man. One day you look up and you are thirty, forty, fifty, sixty and so on. I don't want to be one that looks back and ask myself where did time go and have not done anything I wanted to do. I try to do the things I want to do while I can. Have you ever really and truly thought about this? On the other hand, you probable think that you will never be able to do all the things that you want to do. Guess what? I sure will be trying. All things are possible through Christ who strengthens me. Never feel guilty about being blessed; you deserve it. I have learned the true meaning of being blessed is to bless someone else. God wants us to enjoy the things he has put here for us. It is hard to know who you need to bless and who doesn't ask God for guidance. Some people look and act like they don't have a dime and is blessed more than you are. I can recall a conversation that I had with a seasoned person one time. When I say seasoned, I mean an older person who know about life. This old lady asked me if I was to walk into a lounge for drinks and there were two men sitting at the bar, one man is dressed nice and the other man had on dirty work clothes, which one would you pick? I thought about it for a minute and before I could get my answer out the old lady told me baby always pick the man in the dirty work clothes. It was if she knew my answer. I was going to say the man that is dressed nice. My mouth flew opened and I asked her why would I do that. She said that the well-dressed man probable don't work or won't do much work, all he wants to do is look good. She said that the man in the dirty clothes will work and treat me right. I would have never thought on that accord at that time because I was young. She said to me always be careful of the choices you make to remember to never judge a book by its cover. I did not understand then but oh do I understand now. I have always liked being around older people; they are so full of wisdom. I love hearing them talk about the old days and how they did things back then. When you are going through somethings, they always have good advice. Some people do not have time for older people, but I am the opposite. So many of the old people did not learn to read or write but could tell you what time of the day it is without looking at a clock. God granted them that, he took care of them. I can recall a time when we were sitting looking through some photo albums and my big mama looked at a picture and told us what time it was because the side that our shadow was on. I looked at my big mama with amazement wishing I had some of what she had. Old people are just so amazing to me. If it was not for them, there will be no me or you. They paved the way for us. All it takes is a little patience and a lot of love. I have always remembered what my mom would say to me about being careful how you treat people. She said that we know where we have been, but we do not know where we are going. You never know who will have to give you a drink of water. Oh, how I miss my mom.

My sisters and I have talked about having a sisters weekend for years but have not had one yet. I have wished so many times that we could have had one before my sister Millie transitioned home with Jesus. It was seven girls and five boys. It's now six girls and three boys. I would love for us to start a tradition; time is so valuable, and we need to make good use of it. We are in a pandemic, and I know how things are. Everyone in my circle has ben vaccinated, wearing their masks and doing the things we need to do. I know that it is going to be a while before any of us will be completely comfortable with traveling again. I pray that when this pandemic is over that we will get it started. We need to get to know each other as adults now. Everybody have their way, but we will be okay for one weekend a year. It does not matter if we have to travel near or far just as long as we spend that time together. These are my sisters from the oldest to the youngest: Wilma, Stella, Bell, Millie, Clara, Ashley and myself. Millie is no longer with us, and I miss her so much. These are my brothers from the oldest to the youngest: Pete, Jerry, Russel, Jack and Walter. Jerry and Russel is no longer with us, and I miss them too. The point is, we just don't spend enough time together, we need to do better. I know there will be moments but that is how it is with family. There may even be times when someone will ask themselves why did I agree on coming on this trip? All I have to say is it would not be family if somebody don't do something or say something to get on your nerves because that is what family do. I do believe that we can do a weekend a year together we don't have to go home with each other. I am going to keep pushing for our sister's weekend. Alright sisters where is the love? I love you guys!

I have been single for seventeen years now. I was married twenty-one years between my three husbands. I have been single almost as long as I have been married. I have had my share of relationships that don't go anywhere. I always end up attracting the wrong men in my life. They are always looking for a free ride, something I am not willing to give them. I can not deal with a man that sits and waits on a woman to see what she is going to do. I need a man in my life that is a real man that does what need to be done. I can say that out of my three marriages that two of my husband did what they were suppose to do. The only thing was there was always disagreement and misunderstandings. I have never been one to argue or try to get back at anyone because in the end you only hurt yourself. I have looked at myself because I know that we can be our own worst enemy. I am the kind of woman that likes to get things done. What I mean about that is if something need to be fixed around the house, I don't believe in waiting until he decides to get it fixed. I would hire someone else to do it. That created a lot of problems in one of my marriages. I have been told that I don't give people a chance to do anything. How much time does it take I have waited weeks and sometimes months? I have been ridiculed because of that. What is it about a man that he gets so angry when another man does what he won't do? Being single have its rewards and then again it has its downfalls. The reward is the peace and quiet, I just love my peace and quiet. You do not have to worry about pacifying anyone to get along especially someone that always got some kind of issue. The downfall is the loneliness I experience from time to time. Sometimes you want someone to talk to, someone who cares about what kind of day you had or how you are feeling. Having someone to hold you in their arms and tell you everything is going to be alright. That means a lot to a woman to feel secure and happy. It would be nice to have someone in your life that think about you when they are not with you by picking up something for you while they are out just because. Those are the things that I want in a man; qualities I have longed for all my life. Just small things like watching TV and eating together sometimes not having words to say just enjoying being together. Like I said, there are some downfalls and there are some rewards when the holidays come around and birthdays. Valentine's Day is sweetheart day with no sweetheart. Co-workers getting flowers, candy, teddy bears and balloons that their sweethearts was sending them. On the day after they come in talking about what they did and where they went. They put it up on social media as well for everyone to see. Then I ask myself why I can't have a sweetheart in my life that loves me unconditionally and I him. A man that love God first and me next. I know that if he loves God, he will know how to love me because he will get his guidance from God. I pray for guidance all the time especially to not make any more mistakes when it comes to being in another relationship. I do not have a question in my mind about the love I have for God. I am trusting and believing that He has a soulmate out there somewhere for me. I do believe there are still some good men out there, they are just so hard to find. Those that use to be good men, women have done them so wrong until they don't think there are any good women out here, but I am here.

Looking back on my relationships and marriages, I am not going to say that I did not have faults. I know there are somethings I could have done a little different. I know that I like having things my way sometimes too. When I really think about it, I know that there were two men in my life that I could say loved me in their own selfish way. I have always wanted to know if a person could be in love with two people at the same time. My thought is that you are going to loved one more than the other, but I am no expert on love. In every marriage and relationship that I have been in, I was the one to call it quits. Maybe I should have stuck in there a little longer. I have been told that I had been spoiled by the men that have come through my life. When I think about it, I do not think so. I have been told that is my biggest problem. Sometimes I think to myself maybe I am. I have always gotten my way in every relationship I have been in. That was only because I knew how to approach my mates. There is nothing wrong with that. I will just wait to see what tomorrow brings. I just want to throw up my hands and say forget it I am tired of trying to figure it out. I have been in three marriages and several relationships, and I have not found my soulmate yet. What would you suggest that I do, really? I sometimes look around when I am out, and it seems likes everybody I see have somebody. I don't want to put up with a lot of nonsense or chaos, just to have a body by my side. I don't see me just settling. I feel like I'm better than that. God wants us to have the best and I know the person he will send me will be. My father do not give no junk. That is why I stay steadfast and ready for anything that Satan put in my path. You will be amazed at the things that has come across my pass lately. Just listening to their smooth talk and all the things they think I want to hear. I have had one guy to tell me that I was the hardest woman he ever tried to get through to. There is another guy that stop calling because I did not say what he wanted me to say. I am fine with that because I am always asking God to please don't let those people who do not mean me any good come near me or my dwelling place. I have so often said, I live a peaceful and drama free life. I thank God because he has been doing that for me. I am just not one to fall for anything and pray that I will know my soulmate when I meet him, if I meet him. I am not getting any younger. I just wonder if there are any other ladies out there that feel like I do? For those ladies that are happily married or in good relationships, I really need some pointers from you on how to you do it. I applaud you and pray that everything continue to go well for you. I love seeing a happy couple together, it lets me know that there is hope.

If I could go back and change some things in my life the first thing would be to have spent more time with my mom and other family members that have transitioned from this world. If I known that they were going to be gone so soon, I would have had many more conversations with my mom. It hurt me so the times she would say that she did not want to be a burden to her children. She raised twelve children and we were never a burden to her. If we were, she would have given my uncle some of us. So how could she feel that way even for a minute? I said to mom that she will never be a burden to me because I love you. I really wanted her to know that. I would have done differently when it came to one of my past marriages and maybe one of my relationships. I would have taken a little more time to let them talk and not always wanting to have the last word. I was like that for a while. I was one that did not have much to say until I was tired of what was going on. By this time, I am getting ready to walk or he is. Maybe if I had addressed every issue that came up, but I don't like to argue. I got so tired of arguing until there were times, I did want to be by myself. If I could do it all again, I would have compromised a little more and had more patience. As I think back, I do believe that my first love is the real reason I have been the way I have been in my relationships. He was really so cruel when we broke up. I promised myself when he walked away from me that he would be the last man to walk away from me. I guess I kept that promise because he was the first and the last. I would go back and give them a different me. I put up this brick wall and did not want to tear it down, it was my protection. I ask myself have I really ever opened my heart up all the way to any man.

I also would like to have spent more time with my sister Millie, We spent a lot of time on the phone but it's not the same as being in the presence of each other. We both were looking forward to our trip across county in her RV. I know we would have had a nice time. We wanted all the sisters that could go to go with us as well. We knew that we would never get all of us in one place. I do miss Millie so much. I would have spent more time with my brother Russel also. Due to different circumstances, unfortunately, we did not. If I could do it all over again nothing would have stopped me. Russell had a good heart, and he loved his family. Every chance he got he did come around. I talked to Russel a lot on the phone as well. He did get a chance to do a lot of traveling before he settled down and got married. He was very outgoing in his younger years. Russel loved his wife Oliva, his daughter Madeline, and his grandchildren. I would have also tried to talk my brother Jerry into moving out from the community he was living in. I was young and didn't really know at the time what was going on. Knowing what I know today, I am sure I would have.

Finishing college would have been another thing I would have done. I only have a few hours left to get my degree in Elementary Education. There really is no excuse for me not going back to finish I just never did. Like they say, 'it's never too late.' Who knows what tomorrow will bring? I know someone will say that I might as well forget it at my age. It is about me not them. Through the years and seeing how the certified teacher had so much on them I think is part of the reason I did not go back as well. I have stayed in the Teacher Assistant jobs since August of

1999. I have been a Certified Nursing Assistant since 1985. I have kept myself busy over the years. I just wished I could turn back the hands of time. Unfortunately, it is not going to happen, so I thank God for the life he has allowed me to live this far. I have so often said life is about the choices we make. When my sister Bell and I was in high school, we both went to Home Economics. Bell went to the sewing department, and I went to the cooking department. I have wished many days that I would have gone to the sewing department. I could be making my own clothes and clothes for my grandchildren.

Looking back on life I see a lot that I could have changed. Then I think if I could have changed anything would I be the person I am today? Would I be wiser, happier or what? I think things happened just the way it was supposed to. To those who is reading this, take my advice and live your life to the fullest and never say that you don't deserve it. God wants you to enjoy life just remember to put him first in everything that you do. I pray that some of the things I have talked about in my book has helped someone in some way. May God continue to bless you and yours.